SUCCESSFUL STRATEGIC HUMAN RESOURCE PLANNING

Allan Bandt
Stephen G. Haines

This book is dedicated to my wife and best friend, Moira. Without her life long support and assistance, I would not be consulting in the field I love and enjoying the rich opportunities gained from the clients with whom I work.

Allan Bandt

This book is dedicated to Jesse Daniels and Cliff Urlich, two high level Marriott Corporation HR Executives who had enough faith in me to recommend me for my first Director of HR position, only nine months removed from the U.S. Navy.

Stephen Haines

A Special Thanks

We would also like to acknowledge the work of our colleague and Canadian Managing General Partner, Mr. Jim McKinlay, for his contributions to the development of the "Strategic People Edge Management" model – upon which this book is based.

Thanks, Jim!

Library of Congress Control Number: 2002103081
Bandt, Allan
Haines, Stephen G.
Successful Strategic Human Resource Planning:
Creating Your People as a Competitive Advantage
ISBN 0-9719159-0-3
Printed in Canada

ABOUT THE AUTHORS

***Allan Bandt*—Bandt Gatter and Associates**

Allan is a Director of Bandt Gatter and Associates, a West Australia-based Human Resource Consultancy Service and regional managing partner of the Centre for Strategic Management for all of Australia and New Zealand.

Allan has held Senior Management and Executive positions in Human Resource Management. He is a past President of the Australian Human Resource Institute (WA), and a past National Director of the Australian Human Resource Institute. He was also the National Chair of the Institute's Strategic Planning Committee.

Allan has considerable consulting and training experience in Human Resource Management. He has been responsible for development of Strategic Human Resource Plans, both in the Public and Private Sector in Australia and internationally.

Allan has successfully conducted this workshop in the United States, Canada and Singapore. He is a Partner of the International Centre for Strategic Management, San Diego, a centre of excellence in Systems Thinking and Strategic Human Resource Planning.

***Stephen Haines*—Centre for Strategic Management®**

Steve is the President and founder of the International Centre *for* Strategic Management® with offices in the United States, Canada, Australia, and world-wide (15 offices). Steve is an internationally recognised leader in Strategic Management, Transformational Change, and Strategic Human Resource (HR) Planning, with 25 years of diverse international and executive experience in private and public sectors. He was formerly Executive Vice President of Imperial Corporation of America, a $13 billion nationwide financial services firm, and President and co-owner of University Associates (UA) Consulting and Training Services. Steve has been on eight top management teams with organisation leadership for Human Resources, Training, and Organisational Development. A US Naval Academy Engineering graduate with a Foreign Affairs minor, Steve has a Master's Degree in Organisation Development and has completed his Ed. D. course work (ABD) in Management and Educational Psychology.

He has written eight books, over 60 articles, eight volumes of the Centre's *Tool Kits and Guides* (4000+ pages), and taught over 70 different seminars. He has served on a number of corporate boards and was chairman of a credit union. Steve is in demand as an international keynote speaker on strategic and people issues for Chief Executive Officers and boards-of-directors.

Steve can be reached at:
Centre *for* Strategic Management®
1420 Monitor Road
San Diego, CA 92110-1545
USA
Email: csmintl@san.rr.com
Telephone: (619) 275-6528
Fax: (619) 275-0324

Allan can be reached at:
Bandt Gatter & Associates
2 Lawrence Avenue
West Perth, WA 6005
Australia
Email: bandtgat@opera.iinet.net.au
Telephone: 61-89-322-2877
Fax: 61-89-322-2083

TABLE OF CONTENTS

INTRODUCTION

The Challenge

How often do we utter the phrase, "People are our greatest asset"? Yet, at the same time, we fail to develop an overall systematic approach that strategically aligns and attunes Human Resource Practices with organisational objectives.

For most organisations, the costs dedicated to staff salaries and benefits accounts for the single largest budget expenditure (varying from a low of about 60 percent in a manufacturing setting to a high of about 85 percent in a service organisation). Thus, it makes both good common sense and good business sense to focus time and attention on the development of a Strategic Human Resource/People Management System that creates "The People Edge (or Advantage)" in the marketplace. But what's the best way of doing this?

Through our in-depth Systems Thinking research, we have created a "People Edge *Process* Model" for developing a Strategic Human Resource/People Management Plan. We have also developed a companion "People Edge *Content* Model" for examining the "Six People Edge Best Practices".

The application of our Systems Thinking Approach^{SM} to Strategic Planning and Human Resource Management has led us to look for practical, systematic methods of properly positioning the Human Resource Function in the 21st Century. We should be able to maximize our people management gains for the organisation, employee, customer, shareholder and community.

As a result, we have researched, developed and refined our Strategic People Edge Model over the years to show organisations a straightforward Systems Thinking Approach^{SM} on how to create the People Edge necessary to develop and sustain a competitive business advantage in the Marketplace.

This People Edge approach is outlined in this publication, and we wish you success in its implementation in your organisation.

***Note 1**: The phrase **People Management** is often used throughout this book in preference to the phrase "Human Resource." We do this because the term "Human Resource" is often interpreted as referring to the Human Resource Function—when People Management should be the function and business of everyone, but especially of Senior Management, as you will see.*

***Note 2:** The phrase "Strategic Human Resource (HR)/People Plan" will be used to identify the two different ways this plan can be done. Example: The Human Resource Department Plan or an Organization-wide People Plan.*

SUCCESSFUL
STRATEGIC HUMAN RESOURCE PLANNING

The objectives for this book, *Successful Strategic Human Resource Planning*, are listed below. They have been developed to identify the core issues covered in this book. This book allows you and your team to create and implement the Strategic Human Resource/People Plan on your own, following these steps. You can do it for an HR Department, or for your Organisation, using a cross-sectional slice of management.

Objectives of this Book

To define *Strategic Human Resource/People Planning* and show how to organise it

To explain *Business Scanning* as a way to link people management to business success

To explain *Visioning*, *Measuring* and *Strategising* for people management success

To suggest practical ways to *Implement Strategic Human Resource/People Plan*

Objectives of Strategic Human Resource/People Planning for the Organisation

We have three goals for this process:

Goal #1: Develop the Strategic Human Resource/People Plan/Document and yearly priorities

Goal #2: Ensure successful implementation and change

Goal #3: Build and sustain high performance in people management over the long term

PART I

Step #1: PLAN-TO-PLAN

THE EDUCATING, ORGANISING AND TAILORING STEP

~ PLUS ~

Step #2: BUSINESS SCANNING

ENVIRONMENTAL SCANNING

PHASE 

PHASE E: ENVIRONMENTAL SCANNING

STEP #1:
THE EDUCATING, ORGANISING & TAILORING STEP

Engineering success at the front end of our Strategic HR Planning Process

Every moment spent planning saves 3 - 4 in execution

Strategic Human Resource/People Planning is often poorly accomplished (though not by intent or incompetence) by Human Resource Planners, Managers and others. This is often due to a lack of advance preparation and knowledge: That is why we have introduced *Plan-to-Plan*, Step #1 in the Strategic HR/People Planning Process. Plan-to-Plan is the educating, organising & tailoring step that ensures success up front before getting to the actual development of your Strategic HR/People Management Plan.

Strategic HR/People Planning is a dynamic, backward-thinking process conducted by both senior/line managers and human resource professionals. Such planning is ideally a partnership between all groups. Together they define their Ideal Future of People Management (Vision) for the organisation, and the core strategies necessary to achieve people effectiveness. Based on these strategies they then develop meaningful, annual operating plans and budgets. Then these plans drive the achievement and measurement of the people management vision.

Begin your Strategic HR/People Planning process by conducting a *Plan-to-Plan Day*. Involve your senior executive team; this allows everyone involved in your process to become educated and organised about Strategic HR/People Planning. This first, critical step is often overlooked, with disastrous consequences later on when the planning process or its implementation fails.

Here is how it works:
Set up a one-day meeting with your Planning Team for this *Plan-to-Plan Day*. Plan-to-Plan is the pre-work of the planning process. It is required to determine organisational readiness for planning and is an overall educating, organising and tailoring step. It answers questions such as "who needs to be involved in the planning to ensure ownership?" It also identifies strategic information that management must gather to accomplish the planning process.

A key initial task is to form the Planning Team to provide overall stewardship for the people in the organisation to actually create The Plan (this team is also sometimes called an Executive or Employee Leadership Development Board). It also creates opportunities for the involvement of all key stakeholders in the planning process.

Note*: To order a Strategic HR/People Plan template to make it easier to produce a document, please call or email us, or check our website at* www.csmintl.com.

THE CHANGING FACE OF PEOPLE MANAGEMENT

Human Resource/People Management today is undergoing significant changes, with huge planning, staffing, and implementing implications for Executives, Line Managers and the Human Resource Professionals alike.

Major trends and challenges facing organisations include:

1. ***Technology***
   - Utilizing new technologies (Intranet, etc.) that enable the HR Department to become more cost efficient, and line managers and employees to more effectively carry out their Human Resource responsibilities on their own without HR involvement.

2. ***Demographics***
   - Managing the diverse cultural workforce of Baby Boomers, Generation X'ers, Generation Y'ers and dot com workers—each with their own demands and expectations of the workplace.

3. ***Changing Workplace Dynamics***
   - Developing new ways to motivate, reward and recognize employees. Employees are placing an increased emphasis on individual focus… on personal success, with a resulting loss of employee loyalty to an employer.

4. ***Globalisation***
   - Managing to grow nationally and internationally by utilizing different skills, cultures and approaches to managing organisations, customers and staff, in order to adapt to the changing nature of world economies.

TRENDS & CHALLENGES FOR HUMAN RESOURCE PROFESSIONALS

Human Resource Professionals are being required to act differently in order to meet the people management challenges of this decade:

1. ***Aligning HR Practices***
   - Ensuring the alignment and linkages of all human resource practices to the company's business strategies and stakeholder needs
2. ***Business Partnerships***
   - Working in partnership with line managers and staff to address the people-related business needs of the organisation
3. ***Organisational Change***
   - Facilitating organisational change, cultural change, and learning throughout the organisation
4. ***Technology***
   - Understanding and utilizing state-of-the-art HR technology to increase the efficiency and effectiveness of the organisation
5. ***Strategists***
   - Understanding the diverse environment in which they work and positioning their organisation for the future

EXERCISE:

Individually, list the major human resource challenges and issues facing your organisation. Share your list with the rest of your planning group.

THREE KEY PREMISES

Three key premises underpin all Strategic Human Resource/People Edge Planning. Conduct a meeting with your Planning Team and review these three premises:

Premise 1: Strategic People Edge Management is a Key Part of Good Leadership at Every Level of Management

Any organisation embarking on Strategic Human Resource/People Planning must first decide if the planning is just:

- an event
- a process
- a change in roles
- a change in the way we do our people business

While the complete answer is yes to all of these, Strategic Human Resource/People Planning must culminate in a significant change in the way Human Resource activity is managed within the organisation. This is an essential difference between our Strategic Human Resource Planning Model and most others that end up not getting implemented.

Installing a Strategic Human Resource/People Management ***Structure*** to implement Strategic Human Resource/People Planning and change is the new way to run your people processes.

Strategic Human Resource/People Plans are essentially blueprints. The second step for management and human resource staff is to implement the plans and manage change based on a Strategic Human Resource/People Management Plan and an accompanying Annual Plan and System.

If you don't want anything to change, why bother to plan?

Implementing new human resource practices brings with it new ways of doing work, undertaking tasks and structuring activity. Effective Strategic Human Resource/People Planning involves significant change. Change can be one of the major threats to effective implementation of new human resource strategies. Your organisation must counter the natural human tendency to repeat familiar behaviours and past habits.

Thus, it cannot be stressed too early that Strategic Human Resource/People Planning and Managing Strategic Human Resource Change must be championed consistently and persistently by a single- minded dedication of the leaders doing the planning (both senior line managers and human resource professionals).

Premise 2: "People Support What They Help Create"

Any team, department or organisation's first year of Strategic Human Resource/People Planning involves setting in place the necessary plans, processes and documents. Establish a core planning team of 8-15 people from your collective leadership and key stakeholders. (This should include at minimum senior line managers, human resource executives and human resource staff). A crucial task of the planning team is to hold consensus-building meetings involving the rest of the management, staff, human resource personnel and other stakeholders.

Because people support what they help create, you should not plan in a vacuum. Instead, involve all of the people who matter to you (or who will help with implementation) as you plan. Make sure you work within the framework of your Corporate Strategic Plan if you have one. Gather stakeholder input in separate meetings as each draft document is developed as well as when it is finalized. You will get a host of new and different ideas to improve the quality of your plan. If you wait until you finish Strategic Human Resource/People Planning, others will be less likely to support you in its implementation.

Premise 3: Use Systems Thinking—Focus on Outcomes: Serving Your Customer!

Systems (or Backwards) thinking is a five-phase framework to ***clarify and simplify*** your Human Resource/People Planning and implementation. Earlier versions of Strategic Human Resource/People Planning dealt mostly with the present and forecasted into the future. Today's planning, however, must begin with your future in mind. Why? It is a common-sense notion, just like knowing where you want to end up before you get into your car to drive somewhere.

Careful goal selection is the primary criterion of success in all the literature on organisations, teams, and individuals. This means first establishing a vision of your future, defining your purpose, and stating your mission: then finish your planning.

To create a high-performance organisation, department or team, planning and implementation must fit and work together as a system. The word "system" is, however, often overused and frequently misunderstood. To ensure that we are thinking alike, let's define it.

A system is a set of components that work together for the overall objective of the whole (output).

SYSTEMS THINKING

EXERCISE:

Diagram or draw the elements that describe any system (there are generally agreed to be five such elements). Share your diagram with other members of your team and discuss.

NOW, COMPARE OUR SYSTEM WITH YOURS

THE SYSTEMS THINKING APPROACH[SM]

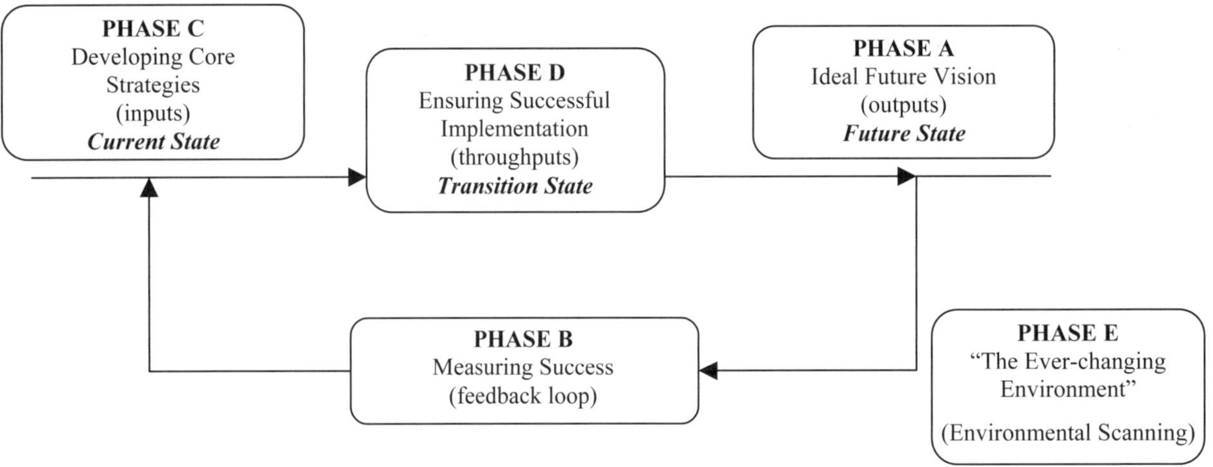

The first four of these elements (ABCD) correspond to the four phases of our strategic planning framework, the fifth being understood as the dynamic and ever-changing environment within which the system operates. We begin at Phase A, the ideal future vision we want to achieve (system output). Then, we work backward to the present and plan the strategies to achieve that vision.

Phase A: ***Output*** defines your ideal future success in your own terms: "Where do we want to be in the future at time X?"

Phase B: ***Feedback loop*** measures key factors and reports on the status of the results.

Phase C: ***Input*** of assessments of where you are today is the primary means to close the "Gap" between today and the Ideal Future gap by means of core strategies that achieve your ideal vision.

Phase D: ***Throughput*** consists of a set of specific yearly priority actions to ensure successful implementation of your plan.

Phase E: ***Environmental Scanning*** is an ongoing process done at least quarterly or semi-annually.

Strategic HR/People Planning must start with the *output* (outcomes, ends, desired results or goals) since we want to be proactive in creating our ideal future for our workforce and work environment. This is what distinguishes Strategic HR/People Planning from traditional, long range, and other forms of planning. Traditional forms of planning usually start with the present-focusing primarily on the problem-solving of existing issues rather than having a vision of success and profitability, and building cascading action plans to achieve it. Traditional planning tends to be a piecemeal, analytical approach to a systems problem. It also fails to address the Plan-to-Implement step, our Step #8 and our implement and change process (Steps #8 - #10).

Phases A, B, C, D and E and their sequences are true *Systems Thinking* and are essential to a high level of success. The following diagram illustrates these five phases and the ten steps (explained in detail in upcoming sections) of successful Strategic HR/People Planning.

The ***"Strategic People Edge Management Model"*** outlined below is based on over five years of solid experience using it with many individuals, teams, departments and organisations in the real world as well as extensive best practices literature research on planning prior to that by the Centre for Strategic Management®.

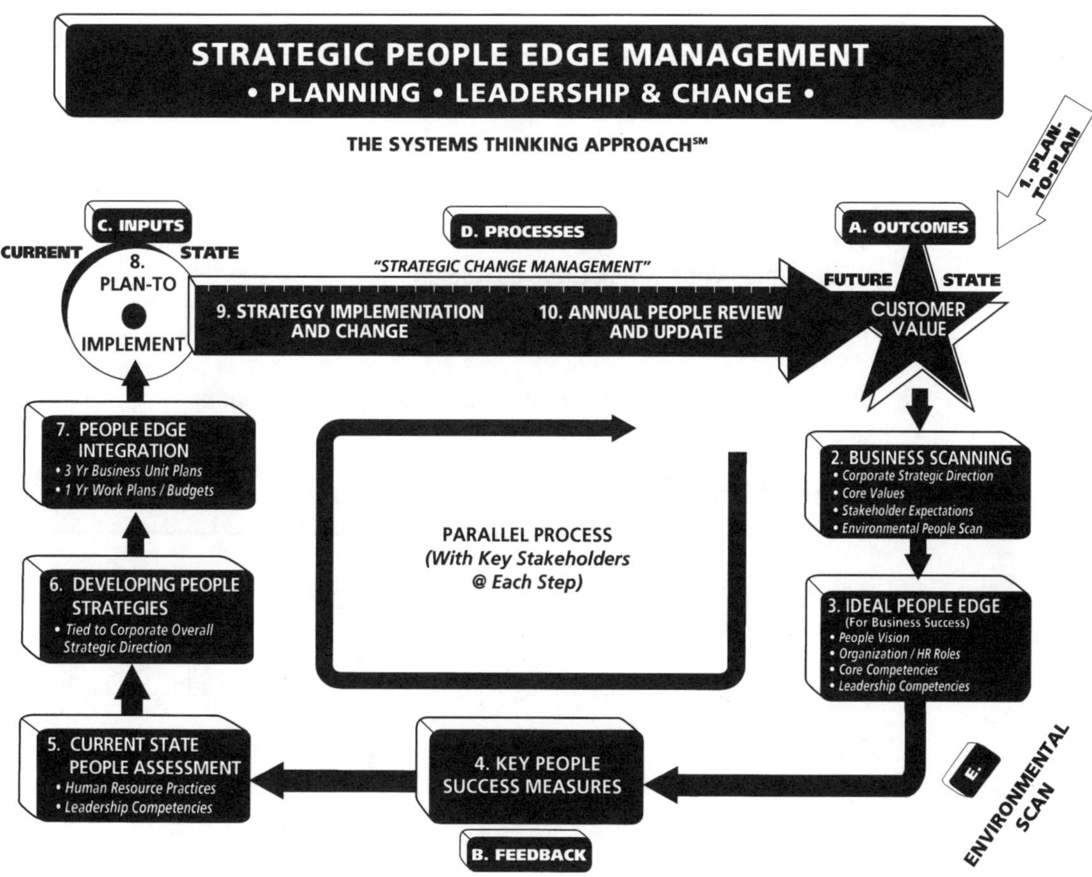

KEY BENEFITS: STRATEGIC HUMAN RESOURCE/PEOPLE MANAGEMENT SYSTEM

Establishing an effective *Strategic Human Resource/People Edge Management System* provides a systematic approach that strategically aligns and attunes human resource Practices with organisational objectives. It is useful, especially for internal marketing purposes, to identify the benefits for your organisation.

EXERCISE:

Which benefits do you want? Check those that are important to you. Compare your results with the rest of your team.

_________ 1. Take a proactive strategic approach to positioning the organisation to maximise your competitive advantage.

_________ 2. Partner with Line Management to solve people-related business issues.

_________ 3. Build a cross-functional approach for dealing with people management issues.

_________ 4. Identify the "high leverage" core people strategies that will provide maximum advantage for your organisation.

_________ 5. Focus human resource practices on outcomes and efficiencies rather than activities and bureaucracy.

_________ 6. Build a quantifiable base for measuring the people value-added benefits.

_________ 7. Provide the basis for intelligent people budget and resource allocation decisions.

_________ 8. Ensure that people strategies are actively executed.

_________ 9. Provide the basis for managed organisational change.

_________ 10. Ensure that everyone is "singing the same tune" in relation to people management within the organisation (i.e., attunement with people's hearts and minds in support of satisfying the customer).

COMMON MISTAKES: STRATEGIC HUMAN RESOURCE/PEOPLE MANAGEMENT SYSTEM

A Strategic Human Resource/People Management System can fail at many points. Identifying some of the common mistakes early in the process can be helpful in making your planning outcomes more successful.

EXERCISE:

Which mistakes do you make or are likely to make? Check the ones that apply.

________ 1. Not even doing any formal people planning

________ 2. Failing to integrate Strategic HR/People Planning at all levels

________ 3. Delegating HR/People Management Planning to the HR staff only

________ 4. Keeping HR/People Management planning separate from day-to-day management

________ 5. Conducting long-range forecasting only

________ 6. Having a scattershot approach to Strategic HR/People Management Planning

________ 7. Developing vision, mission and value statements as fluff

________ 8. Failing to use strategic information and analysis to drive the plan

________ 9. Failing to take into account the needs of all key stakeholders—employees, customers and investors

________ 10. Failing to identify the critical business issues and competency requirements as a basis for driving the strategic plan

COMMON MISTAKES: STRATEGIC HUMAN RESOURCE/PEOPLE MANAGEMENT SYSTEM

________	11. Failing to complete an effective implementation process, including not focusing on the "critical few" areas
________	12. Conducting business as usual after Strategic Human Resource/People Planning (**S**trategic **P**eople **P**lan **O**n **T**op **S**helf ((**SPOTS**)) Syndrome)
________	13. Not having line management lead in the development of the plan
________	14. Lacking a scoreboard: Measuring what is easy, not what is important
________	15. Lacking a balanced scoreboard approach—i.e., measuring financial, customer, business process and employee measures
________	16. Neglecting to benchmark yourself against the competition
________	17. Seeing the planning document as an end in itself
________	18. Trying to facilitate the process yourself
________	19. Violating the *"people support what they help create"* premise
________	20. Failing to identify the "key leverage points" that will result in the greatest strategic change
________	21. Failing to integrate strategies in the implementation process
________	22. Failing to make the "tough people choices"

Please share your evaluation of planning mistakes with your Planning Team. As a team, problem-solve to correct or avoid these common mistakes.

THE CHANGING NATURE OF THE HR FUNCTION

The biggest challenge facing any organisation that undertakes the development of a "People Edge Plan" is a philosophical and psychological one. The shift that is needed to move from the more traditional concept of Human Resource Management, that has been practiced in many organisations for decades, to that of a Human Resource Management practice designed to meet the needs of the new workplace, is a significant one.

There will be two groups of people who will probably be impacted more than others within your organisation, as you move forward with this change:

- The staff of the Corporate Human Resource Department
- The Line Managers throughout your organisation

ROLE SHIFT FOR HUMAN RESOURCE PROFESSIONALS

Traditionally, Human Resource Professionals have been concerned with the day-to-day administration of the technical nature of the Human Resource function. They have typically played a primary legal, administrative, and service delivery function, including recruitment and staffing, job classification, compensation and benefits, labour relations and contract negotiations, management of personnel records, and career development, as well as staff training and development.

In this role, Human Resource departments have assumed total responsibility for most of these functions. This has been was at the expense of allowing managers to fulfill these direct administrative roles as part of their own responsibility for the people management of their own staff groups.

In the new workplace scenario, Human Resource staffs are expected to play a more significant role from a strategic perspective. They should facilitate, guide and support the corporation's human resource component. These new responsibilities will require Human Resource staff to relinquish many of their current areas of responsibility to line departments and line managers, and instead, provide them coaching and consulting support.

Human Resource staff must be ready to take a legitimate seat at the corporate strategic executive table and concentrate on the areas of people strategies, succession planning, advising, competency development, sharing intellectual capital, and developing techniques to ensure that the corporation's "people edge" becomes their organisation's strategic advantage.

Human Resource staff must be ready to understand and demonstrate how the Human Resource component directly adds value to creating organisational success.

ROLE SHIFT FOR LINE MANAGERS

Originally, before the arrival of HR Professionals, managers were totally responsible for the Human Resource function within their own work group. As more and more of these Human Resource functions were centralised, managers lost focus on these competency areas and "let Human Resources look after it." Those days are quickly coming to a close, if they haven't already disappeared in your organisation.

In the new workplace scenario, managers are expected to re-skill themselves in the technical aspects of the day-to-day Human Resource administrative functions. While they may seek coaching guidance and direction from the Human Resource staff, they will be expected to accept responsibility for:

- Recruitment and selection
- Determining the appropriate level of compensation provided to staff
- Meeting the training and development needs of staff by locating appropriate learning opportunities
- Handling labour issues and grievances at the local level, for the most part

There will still be some HR roles that will remain the responsibility of the Corporate Human Resource Department, such as contract negotiations, benefits administration, payroll, etc. Whether these services are provided directly by the Human Resource Department, or they are provided through some form of *outsourcing agreement*, they will fall outside of the role the Line Manager. In either case, the future role of the Human Resource Department will be significantly different than it was a year ago—and this also applies to line managers.

Managers will need to seek facilitation support and counselling from Human Resource Staff to develop the competencies needed to fulfill these new roles in a way that is compatible and consistent with the corporate strategic plan. They may also require direct support from HR, as a partner, in handling difficult cases.

Managers will be expected to add "People Management" to their job function and learn how to effectively lead people toward becoming their organisation's most valuable and indispensable resources.

TYPES OF STRATEGIC HUMAN RESOURCE PLANS

The term *Strategic Human Resource Planning* can mean different things to different people. We suggest that it is important for you to be clear about what sort of planning you have in mind when you develop a Strategic Human Resource Plan. We have identified two different types of strategic human resource plans that you might consider.

#1 **Strategic People Plan**

This is an organisation-wide, overall People Plan to develop business-related people strategies to achieve the organisation's goal of *People as a Competitive Edge* for Business Success.
This approach is the preferred focus of this workbook.

#2 **Strategic Human Resource Divisional Strategic Plan**

This is the strategic and operating plan for the Human Resource Division or Department as a business unit. It usually has a three-year orientation. Its goal is to support the organisation's People and/or Strategic Plan (and not vice-versa!) Its focus is much more dependent upon the Human Resource function rather than the organisation.

You can initially develop a Strategic Human Resource Plan just for the Human Resource Department. This is a way of learning and getting started, but it is always desirable to develop an organisation-wide Strategic People Plan (#1 above) over time.

COMPLETING THE PLAN-TO-PLAN

When commencing Strategic Human Resource/People Planning, many Human Resource professionals and planners do not devote sufficient time to the preparatory work and information gathering necessary to make the planning process effective. They also fail to gather the necessary environmental information upon which to make strategic decisions. To address this lack of pre-planning we have earlier introduced into our Strategic Human Resource Planning Model Step #1, the concept of Plan-to-Plan. Here we complete Step #1.

EXECUTIVE/EMPLOYEE DEVELOPMENT BOARD (EDB) CONCEPT

1. **Purpose**: To proactively manage and create the organisation's People Edge
2. **Number of EDBs**: Using the linking pin concept.
   I. 1st level
   "Executive EDB"
   II. 2nd level
   4 "SVP EDBs"

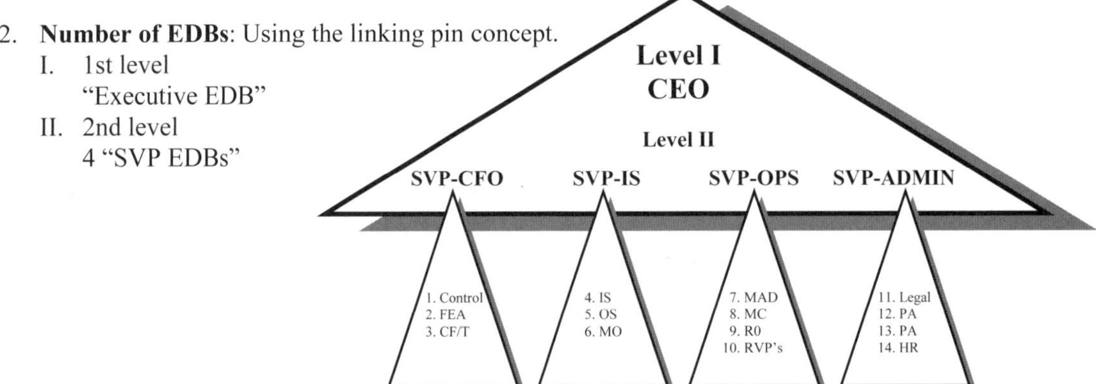

3. **Management of Each EDB (Levels I and II)**
   - Chair
     — Senior officer responsible for stewardship of area
     — Manage the EDB
     — Links to higher level EDB
     — Responsible for EDB decisions/actions/follow-up
   - Members
     — Direct reports of each Chair
     — Responsible for succession presentations
     — Must wear a corporate hat in the meetings for them to be successful
     — Represent their employees as well
   - Secretary/HR Rep
     — Provides content input
     — Ensures employee fair treatment
     — Handles minutes and logistics
     — Ensures process properly occurs as desired
     — Is the linkage person, laterally, to EDBs
     — Provides continual follow-up on EDB desired actions
4. **Meetings**: As necessary, but initially on a quarterly or monthly basis, depending on the rollout of tasks
5. **Rollout**: Recommend initially that only Executive EDB's be established so that officers can gain experience with the process prior to involving Directors.

INVEST IN YOUR PEOPLE FIRST

The people management practices of any organisation should be viewed as a system of people flow from hiring, through their careers, and through retirement and/or termination. (See the Centre's copyrighted HR Systems Model and assessment tools.) Making this all happen is the responsibility of senior management; usually this is best done through an "EDB" (Executive/Employee Development Board) focused solely on this framework and "creating people as a competitive business advantage" *(the People Edge).*

As a Board, this reinforces senior management's responsibility to carry out your "stewardship" responsibilities towards yourselves and the rest of your employees.

The best way to carry this out is to conduct a Strategic "People Edge" Plan to fully define and implement your corporate Strategic Plan's People Strategy.

In essence, this Executive Stewardship Board is responsible for the Human Resource Management flow and continuity. It is executives' responsibility to link staffing to business strategy via:

- Hiring
- Selection (up/lateral)
- Succession planning/core competencies
- Rewards/performance system
- Training: classroom (internal, external)
- Employee surveys of satisfaction/360° feedback
- Organisation design/structure
- Socio-demographic trends
- Developmental jobs/experiences
- Leadership Development System
- Workforce planning

A mechanism/structure of how to achieve management continuity is needed (i.e., a linking pin of Boards):

1. Executive Development Board (EDB)—executive team
2. Management Development Board (MDB)—all department heads/teams
3. Employee Development Committees (EDC)—all supervisors/section head areas

The desired outcomes include:

Right person—Right job—Right time—Right organisation—Right skills!

Sample Monthly Executive Meetings

Week 1	Operational/Business Issues
Week 2	Strategic Planning and Change Process/Status
Week 3	Strategic Change Issues
Week 4	Customer Satisfaction
*Week 5	Executive/Employee Development Board (EDB)
(Quarterly)	Staff, promotion, succession, development
	— HR Executive as secretary to Senior Management

10 KEY TASKS IN THE PLAN-TO-PLAN PROCESS

1. Define the purpose and components of the Strategic Human Resource/People Plan.
2. Gain commitment from the Chief Executive Officer and Senior Executives.
3. Identify the complete Planning Team.
4. Determine time commitment.
5. Educate the Planning Team.
6. Identify the planning information required.
7. Determine who needs to be consulted and kept informed.
8. Identify the Key Stakeholders.
9. Organise administrative support.
10. Determine where the planning task should take place.

PLAN-TO-PLAN CHECKLIST

EXERCISE:

In order to ensure proper pre-planning in your own Strategic Human Resource/People Plan answer the following questions. Compare your findings with those of the rest of your team or a close colleague.

1. Which Strategic Human Resource/People Plan do you want to develop?

   _____ Strategic People Plan for the organization

   _____ Strategic Human Resource Plan for the HR Department

2. Rate the degree of commitment, especially from the CEO or Human Resource Director or other senior line managers, to the plan.

CEO / Executive Director:	High	Medium	Low
Head of Human Resources	High	Medium	Low
Other Key Line Executives	High	Medium	Low

3. List the people who should be part of the Planning Team.

1.	______________	9.	______________
2.	______________	10.	______________
3.	______________	11.	______________
4.	______________	12.	______________
5.	______________	13.	______________
6.	______________	14.	______________
7.	______________	15.	______________
8.	______________	16.	______________

4. List what should be done to prepare or educate the Planning Team.

Read this book?	Y	N
Undertake an Executive Briefing Session (with an outside facilitator)	Y	N

Note: *Contact the Centre for Strategic Management® in the United States or Australia to arrange for an Executive Briefing or consulting support.*

5. Identify key information needs to be gathered in advance.

Corporate Strategic Plan	Y	N
Customer Survey	Y	N
Staffing Information (e.g., turnover rates)	Y	N

6. Check who needs to be consulted as a Key Stakeholder (e.g., customers, employees).

Senior Executive	Y	N
Employees	Y	N
Line Managers	Y	N

7. Check what administrative support and/or equipment will be is required?

Overhead projector & screen	Y	N
Word processor	Y	N
Electronic whiteboard	Y	N
Flip charts	Y	N
Break-out rooms	Y	N

8. Check who needs to be consulted and kept informed?

Employees	Y	N
Executives	Y	N
Line Management	Y	N

9. What parts of the A-B-C-D-E Planning Model will you conduct?

A
- ______ Employee Development Board
- ______ Ideal Future Vision
- ______ HR Department Mission
- ______ Core Values for the Organisation

B
- ______ People Success Measures

C ______ Current State Assessment
______ Core Strategy Development
______ HR Department Three-Year Business Plan
______ Annual Action Priorities under each Core Strategy
______ Re-budget
______ Plan-to-Implement

D ______ Change Steering Committee

E ______ Business Scanning
______ Environmental Scanning

10. What amount of time should be available to complete the planning task?

 2 days
 4 days
 6 days
 other ______________________

11. Outline where you think the planning task should take place? (We recommend off-site)

 Offsite ______________________________

 In-house ______________________________

STEP #2:
BUSINESS SCANNING

One of the criticisms of the Human Resource staff within organisations is that they often do not sufficiently respond to the business-related needs of the organisation. This is one of the reasons we have introduced the Business Scanning step into our planning process. *Business Scanning* is the identification of the corporation's key business strategies and future direction with its people-related implications. It also involves the identification of the core values of the corporation, key stakeholder expectations and the analysis of key environmental issues.

Successful Human Resource practice ensures the alignment of people management strategies with the strategic direction of the business. This helps lead to business success and also establishes Human Resources as a true business partner within the organisation.

Sources of Input in the Business Scanning Process

There are at least five core sources of data to include in the business scanning process:

- The strategic and business direction of the organisation
- The core values of the organisation
- The core competence of the organisation
- Stakeholders expectations
- Key Human Resource issues

EXERCISE

With your group, list the key sources of input that you would use to undertake business scanning for your own Strategic Human Resource Plan.

Information Required	How to gather the information?	Who will gather it?
1. Corporate Strategic Plan		
2. Organisational Environmental Scan		
3. Organisational values		
4. Customer Surveys		
What else?		
5.		
6.		
7.		

EXERCISE: Business Scanning Worksheet

With your group, answer the following business scanning questions.

1. **Environmental Issues**
   What are the key environmental issues impacting our organisation (that may have people management implications)?

2. **Business Strategy**
   What are the key business strategies that our organisation is pursuing during the next two – three years (that may have people management implications)?

3. **Core Values**
   What are the key values of our organisation that need to be built upon in our Strategic Human Resource/People Plan (that may have people management implications)?

4. **Distinctive Competence**
   What are the key things that we need to do exceptionally well as an organisation in order to maintain our competitive advantage (that may have people management implications)?

5. **Stakeholder Issues**
   What are our key stakeholders "People Management" concerns and issues (that may have people management implications)?

6. **Organisation Skills**
   What are the key areas of capability that our workforce needs in order to achieve our business strategy?

7. **Human Resource Issues**
   What are the critical Human Resource issues facing our organisation (that are limiting our success)?

PART II

DEVELOPING
A
STRATEGIC HUMAN RESOURCE
OR PEOPLE PLAN
AND
DOCUMENT

PHASES **A** **B** **C**

PHASE A: CREATING YOUR IDEAL FUTURE

STEP #3:
DEVELOPING THE PEOPLE EDGE IDEAL FUTURE VISION

Plan-to-Plan and ***Business Scanning*** (phase E) are the necessary preparatory steps for the planning process. Step #3 is now the place to actually begin your Strategic Human Resource/People Planning. Based upon our Systems Thinking Approach^{SM} of starting with the outcome first, developing *The People Edge Ideal Future Vision* is the first planning task. It results in an inspirational statement describing where the organisation wishes to be positioned to maximise its people as a competitive advantage. This may also include the articulation of the respective roles of management, of employees, and of the Human Resource function in contributing to organisational success.

Step #3 reinforces the essential principle of linking people practices to the strategic direction of the organisation.

The major challenges in Step #3 are to:

Challenge #1 Develop a **People Edge Ideal Future Vision Statement**—a picture of what you would like your workforce and work environment to be like and look like in the future.

Challenge #2 **Outline the changing roles** of Line Managers, Employees and Human Resource Professionals in People Management Functioning.

Challenge #3 Draft a **HR Department Mission Statement**—why Human Resource exists and what is the value-added contribution of the Human Resource Function to the organisation (i.e., what business it's in and whom it serves).

Challenge #4 **Articulate the Core Organisational Values** (if not already in existence)—that is, identify the core values for the organisation that will guide day-to-day people management and collectively help create your desired organisational culture.

The People Management Vision Statement needs to be:

- Inspirational
- Challenging
- Reflect the changing and contemporary nature of Strategic Human Resource Planning
- Respond to the expectations of Stakeholders
- Support the strategic direction and values of the organisation.

CHALLENGE # 1:
DEVELOPING YOUR PEOPLE EDGE IDEAL FUTURE VISION

EXERCISE:

Instructions:

List your ideas about what your workforce and workforce environment should be like and look like 3-5 years from now.

Instructions:

Share your ideas with a three- or four-person sub-group, or directly with the entire Planning Team. Develop a consensus for a set of concepts for your organisation's People Management Vision Statement.

Hint: Often it is important to first list a set of bullet statements for each concept that the entire group can agree upon.

EXERCISE: (continued)

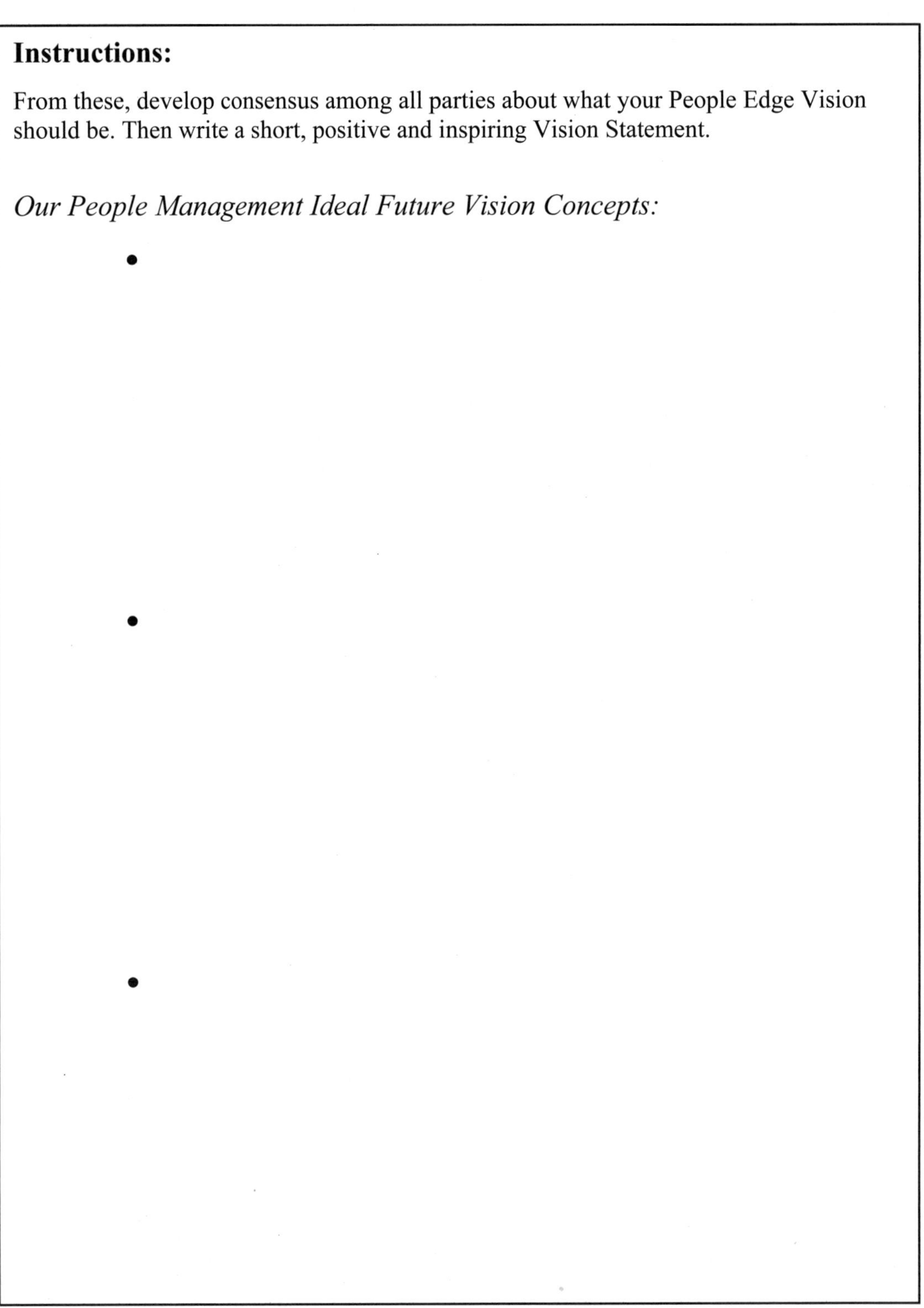

Instructions:

From these, develop consensus among all parties about what your People Edge Vision should be. Then write a short, positive and inspiring Vision Statement.

Our People Management Ideal Future Vision Concepts:

-
-
-

“SAMPLE” PEOPLE EDGE VISION STATEMENT

By the Year 2005, our organisation will have a world-class workforce, known for its delivery of world-class service.

We will be known for a workforce that:

- *Excels in innovation and creativity*
- *Is multi-skilled, team-focused, and operating as an integrated workforce*
- *Is empowered to make decisions in the best interests of our customers*
- *Exploits the use of technology in all of its practices*

Our staff will be working in an environment where:

- *Valuing people and recognising them is part of our everyday practice*
- *Unnecessary, bureaucratic HR processes that interfere with our business have been eliminated*
- *We are generating value for our shareholders through our people*

CHALLENGE # 2:
OUTLINING CHANGING ROLES IN PEOPLE MANAGEMENT

"People management in organisations is everyone's business!"

The changing nature of the workplace has placed much greater emphasis upon employees being responsible for their own development; for managers to take greater responsibility for their own employees, and for Human Resource staffs to become more strategic and business-like in their approach.

EXERCISE:
Determining People Management Roles

List below the current key people management roles for each of the following groups within your organisation.

CURRENT ROLES

Human Resource Department	Senior Executives
• • • • • • •	• • • • • • •
Employees	**Line Managers**
• • • • • • •	• • • • • • •

EXERCISE: (continued)

Determining People Management Roles

Study the list of key people management roles developed by the Centre for Strategic Management. Compare it with the list that you generated on the preceding page. Consider any that you may have missed.

SAMPLE ROLES

Human Resource Department	**Senior Executives**
• Acts as a strategic partner • Provides leadership • Is a consultant to all • Trains and coaches • Facilitates and advises	• Offer stewardship and modelling • Provide visible leadership • Set policy/direction • Responsible • Accountable
Employees	**Line Managers**
• Take the initiative • Manage themselves and their development • Are empowered by management • Are responsible for self-improvement	• Manage people issues • Teach and develop • Train and coach • Facilitate • Resolve conflict

EXERCISE: (continued)

Determining People Management Roles

As a Planning Team, reach consensus on the key people management roles for your own organisation, and list below:

FINAL PEOPLE MANAGEMENT ROLES DETERMINED

Human Resource Department	Senior Executives
• • • •	• • • •
Employees	**Line Managers**
• • • •	• • • •

CHALLENGE # 3:
DRAFTING A HUMAN RESOURCE DEPARTMENT MISSION STATEMENT

EXERCISE:
A Mission Statement for the Human Resource Department:

The Mission statement outlines the core business of the Human Resource Department within the organisation. It addresses:

- What business you want the Human Resource function to be in (versus the activities you perform today)?
- What is the value-added contribution of the Human Resource Department in meeting the People Edge Vision of the organisation?

Effective Human Resource Department Mission Statements should address the following four questions:

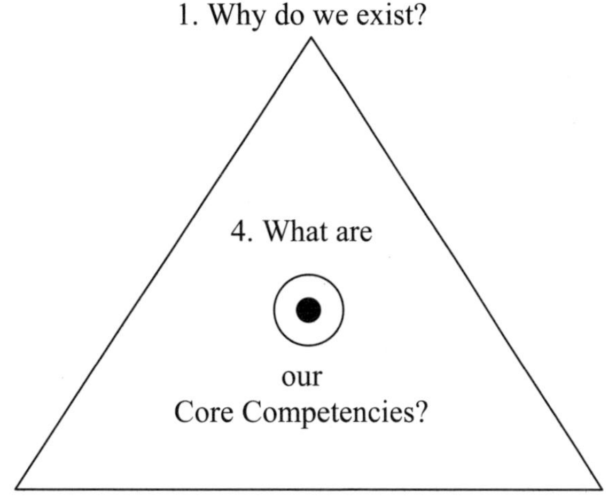

EXERCISE:
Developing the Human Resource Department Mission Statement

Individual Work
Complete this exercise individually. Don't worry about getting the perfect words yet. Just get your key concepts down on paper. Note that question 1, "Why do we exist?" links back to your People Edge Vision Statement. Answer the questions for the way you want to be in the future in year _____________ (end of the planning horizon).

1. *Why do we exist?*
2. *Whom do we serve?*
3. *What do we produce as outcome benefits (i.e., what is our value-added)?*
4. *What should be our Core Competencies in the 21st Century?*

EXERCISE: (continued)
Developing the Human Resource Department Mission Statement

Subgroup Work
Meet in subgroups or as a total planning team, and/or with key stakeholders and agree on your answers to the following four questions. Below your answers, list the key concepts of your Mission Statement.

1. *Why do we exist?*
2. *Whom do we serve?*
3. *What do we produce as outcome benefits (i.e., what is our value-added)?*
4. *What should be our Core Competencies in the 21st Century?*

EXERCISE: (continued)
Developing the Human Resource Department Mission Statement

Final Human Resource Department Mission Statement

Now write your Planning Team's Human Resource Department Mission Statement. It should be:

- Feasible, understandable and concise
- Broad, and continuing in nature, but not so broad as to be meaningless
- Stated in terms of output (results) rather than activities (inputs or throughputs)
- Worded specifically and purposefully (especially the names of your customers, products and services)

Remember that the Mission Statement needs to define the value-added nature of the Human Resource function as it relates to your Key Stakeholders within and outside the organisation.

HUMAN RESOURCE DEPARTMENT MISSION STATEMENT

CHALLENGE #4:
ARTICULATING CORE VALUES

Core values guide our day-to-day behaviours and collectively create the desired culture of the organisation. Sometimes called our beliefs and philosophies, they are few in number and usually meet the following criteria:

- They form a collective organisation-wide belief. While individual values can be different, an organisation requires values shared as a unit.
- They determine the norms or standards of acceptable behaviour concerning how to approach your work.
- They are enduring and consistent over time. They are one of the last things you would want to give up (even in difficult times).
- They are driven by, and crystallised from, the top leadership in the organisation.

The Strategic Human Resource/People Plan should not have a set of separate values from the organisational ones (in fact they should be the same or be supporting of the organisational ones that you are using). However, there may be some additional values identified that should be included in the organisation's core value set.

SAMPLE

Additional Values for the Human Resource Department

- Acting with integrity and transparency in all that we do
- Anticipating and surpassing our customer's expectations
- Working in partnership with line managers to address the business related issues of the organisation
- Being strategic in our approach – always positioning the organisation for the future

EXERCISE:
Developing Human Resource Department Values

List the Organisation's Core Values, as they exist now.

CURRENT CORE VALUES

EXERCISE: (continued)

Developing Human Resource Department Values

Organisational Values Exercise (optional)

("Guides to Behaviour")

Complete **Column #1** (*The Way It Should Be*): Select 10 of the following Values most important to your organisation's future success.
Complete **Column #2** (*The Way It Is Now*) at a later time (or as directed).

Column #1 The way you think it should be ideally	**Column #2** **The way it is now (can also be ideal)**		
________	________	1.	Adaptation to Change
________	________	2.	Long Term Strategic Perspective/Direction
________	________	3.	Energizing/Visionary Leadership
________	________	4.	Risk Taking
________	________	5.	Innovation/Creativity
________	________	6.	Marketplace Aggressiveness/Competitiveness
________	________	7.	Teamwork/Collaboration
________	________	8.	Individual/Team/Organisation Learning
________	________	9.	Recognition of Achievements
________	________	10.	Waste Elimination/Wise Use of Resources
________	________	11.	Profitability/Cost Conscious
________	________	12.	Quality Products/Services
________	________	13.	Customer Service Excellence/Focus
________	________	14.	Speed/Responsiveness
________	________	15.	Continuous/Process Improvement
________	________	16.	Growth/Size of Organisation/Revenue
________	________	17.	Contribution to Society/Community
________	________	18.	Safety
________	________	19.	Stability/Security
________	________	20.	Ethical and Legal Behaviour
________	________	21.	High Staff Productivity/Performance
________	________	22.	Employee Development/Growth/Self-Mastery
________	________	23.	Dialogue/Openness and Trust
________	________	24.	Constructive Confrontation/Problem Solving
________	________	25.	Respect/Caring for Individuals/Relationships
________	________	26.	Quality of Work Life/Morale
________	________	27.	High Staff Satisfaction
________	________	28.	Employee Self-Initiative/Empowerment
________	________	29.	Participative Management/Decision Making
________	________	30.	Data-Based Decisions
________	________	31.	Diversity and Equality of Opportunity
________	________	32.	Partnerships/Alliances
________	________	33.	Excellence in All We Do

Adapted from: S. Haines, *"Internal Sun Co., Inc. Working Paper,"* 1979; J.W. Pfeiffer, L.D. Goodstein, T.M. Nolan, *"Applied Strategic Planning: A How to Do It Guide,"* Pfeiffer & Co., San Diego, CA, 1986; T. Rusk, *"Ethical Persuasion Working Paper,"* 1989; and client feedback ever since.

EXERCISE: (continued)

Developing Human Resource Department Values

Individually, list the People Management Values you want to include in your Human Resource Department Plan.

INDIVIDUAL WORK (optional)

EXERCISE: (continued)

Gaining consensus on your Human Resource Department Values

As a Planning Team, gain consensus on the Core Values for your Human Resource Department. List them below.

FINAL ADDITIONAL HR DEPARTMENT VALUES (optional)

PHASE B: FEEDBACK LOOP

STEP #4:
KEY PEOPLE SUCCESS MEASURES

One of the frequent criticisms of Strategic Human Resource/People Plans is their inability to measure the outcomes of their interventions and actions, and their failure to demonstrate their value-adding contribution to employees, the business, shareholders and the community.

Here we establish the high-level, quantifiable outcome measures that will be used to measure employee success in adding value to our internal customers, shareholders and the community. Outcome measures enable you to answer these questions:

1. How do you know if you are being successful in your Human Resource/People Strategies?
2. How do you know if you are going to get into trouble?
3. If you are off course (in trouble), what corrective action should be taken to get your Strategic Human Resource/People Plan and organisation back on track to achieve your Ideal Future People Edge Vision?

We have identified four key areas for measuring the impact of Key HR/People Strategies:

1. Strategic Perspective	The extent to which the HR/People strategies are positioning the organisation for the future as a "competitive edge"
2. Customer Perspective	The extent to which HR/People Strategies are meeting the needs of the customer groups (internal or external)
3. Internal Process Perspective	The quality and efficiency of internal HR management processes
4. Financial Perspective	Whether the organisation's HR/People Strategy, implementation and execution are contributing to the bottom-line financial improvement of the organisation

KEY PEOPLE SUCCESS MEASURES – SOME TIPS

1. Wherever possible, focus on outputs rather than inputs. Identify the "critical few" indicators of highest leverage.

2. Wherever possible, involve key executives in the shaping of the Key People Success Indicators.

3. Ensure that your indicators are measurable and quantifiable.

4. Set targets/goals for the last year of the planning period.

5. Set baseline measures of where you are today.

6. Set targets or goals for each future year in a "continuous improvement" mode.

7. Key People Success Measures are your "report card." Ensure that the results are made visible to all key stakeholders.

8. Limit yourself to no more than 10 measures. In strategy "less is more."

EXERCISE:
Identifying your Key People Success Indicators—Checklist

Individual Work
Individually, circle the bullets below on those Key People Success Indicators that may be useful in your Strategic Human Resource/People Plan

Key Areas	Measurement Indicators
1. Financial Perspective.	▪ Employee costs in relation to total revenue ▪ Total Health Care costs in relation to number of employees ▪ Turnover costs (termination, hiring costs, etc.) ▪ Revenue growth ▪ Total compensation and benefit cost against revenue
2. Strategic Perspective	▪ Number of positions covered by a plan with a ready successor in place ▪ Percentage of targeted work areas that have projections of future work force needs in place ▪ Percentage of executive development training based upon business needs
3. Customer Perspective	▪ Level of staff turnover ▪ Number of external customer complaints related to employee attitude and behaviour ▪ Percentage of staff that rate the organisation as a positive place to work ▪ Percentage of HR staff that are perceived by managers to have an understanding of the business of the (internal) customers they service ▪ Percentage of managers who feel that they have sufficient HR data and support to make decisions ▪ Percentage of HR expense against total operating expense ▪ Response time taken to respond to line manager requests for service
4. Internal Process Perspective	▪ Average number of days taken to fill a vacant position ▪ Percentage of new recruits performing satisfactorily after six months ▪ Cost per external hire ▪ Extent of HR management information available to staff and managers online

EXERCISE: (continued)

Identifying Additional Key People Success Indicators

More Individual Work

Individually, list any other Key People Success Indicators that you would use to measure the effectiveness of your Strategic Human Resource/People Plan.

EXERCISE: (continued)

Reaching Group Consensus on your Key People Success Indicators

Group Work

As a Planning Team, reach consensus on your Key People Success Indicators. List them below.

FINAL KEY PEOPLE SUCCESS INDICATORS

MEASURING AND TRACKING SUCCESS

Your People Management Report Card

Once the Key People Success Indictors are identified, be sure to set specific measurements and yearly targets. By limiting the number of measures to no more than 10, you will focus on what really is important to your notion of People Management success. A lack of focus is the main problem in almost all types of Strategic Human Resource/People Planning. Key People Success Measures should always measure what is really important (not just what is easy to measure).

Typical customer satisfaction areas might include product quality, service, cost and value, speed and response time, as well as being environmentally responsive.

It is crucial to this step that you understand the different and innovative ways you can measure almost anything. In the absence of clearly defined targets, we are forced to concentrate on activities and efforts only, and ultimately we become enslaved by them.

Key People Success Measures must be specific and quantifiable measures in one of four ways:

- Quality (as perceived by the customer)
- Quantity (production numbers or rates; the presence or absence of a program, etc)
- Time
- Cost

These quantifiable measures will determine your success.

EXERCISE:

Setting Measurable Outcomes

For each indicator that defines people success, set a measurable outcome or target for the final year in your planning horizon. This should be a realistic target that you are deeply committed to achieving. Focus on the vital few outputs, not the many trivial activities. The operative concept is key not comprehensive success factors.

Key Success Measures					
Key Success Indicator	Baseline Year _____ Target	Year 1 _____	Year 2 _____	Year 3 _____	Planning Horizon Year _____ Target

PHASE C: INPUTS

CONVERTING STRATEGIES TO ACTION

A consistent theme in all strategic and people management planning processes is that successful organisations are those that not only develop vision and direction, but are also relentless in their implementation and execution of strategies.

Phase C of the Human Resource/People Management Planning Model takes stock of current conditions and the status of our Human Resource functioning today. We then establish core strategies—including a set of priority actions for the next year—to close the gap. These core strategies become the organising framework to guide the rest of your Strategic Human Resource/People Planning process—from the Strategic Human Resource/People Plan—to the annual Operational Plan—to the individual level of action and accountability.

STEP #5:
CURRENT STATE PEOPLE ASSESSMENT

While there are many ways to conduct an organisational assessment, the most clear and simple way is to conduct an analysis of your internal **S**trengths and **W**eaknesses, and your external **O**pportunities and **T**hreats. Then, examine the gaps between this analysis and the organisations vision for strategic and action implications. This is often called a *SWOT Analysis.*

Undertaking a Current State People Assessment

If you are doing this analysis for the people practices or as part of a larger organisation, keep in mind that "external" means outside of your organisation. If you are doing this analysis for a Human Resource Department there are <u>two</u> externals, one inside and one outside of your area within the larger organisation. You may, therefore, decide to complete two external analyses.

Over the next three pages, complete a SWOT Analysis of your current situation; review it with a sub-group - the whole planning team - and finally your key stakeholders. Make additions or corrections as necessary. You may find that some issues have both strengths and weaknesses, or that some offer both threats and opportunities.

EXERCISE:
SWOT Analysis—Organisational

Fill in your own analysis of your Organisation's people Strengths, Weaknesses, Opportunities and Threats.

Internal People Analysis	
Strengths ("Build")	**Weaknesses ("Eliminate/Cope")**
1.	1.
2.	2.
3.	3.
4.	4.
5.	5.
6.	6.
7.	7.
8.	8.
9.	9.
10.	10.
External People Analysis	
Opportunities ("Exploit")	**Threats ("Ease/Lower")**
1.	1.
2.	2.
3.	3.
4.	4.
5.	5.
6.	6.
7.	7.
8.	8.
9.	9.
10.	10.

EXERCISE: (continued)
Final SWOT Analysis—Gaining Consensus

Once you have completed your individual thoughts on your Organisation's current state people analysis, review it with the whole planing team - and finally your key stakeholders. Make additions or corrections as necessary on this page and the next.

Internal People Analysis	
Strengths ("Build")	**Action**
1.	1.
2.	2.
3.	3.
4.	4.
5.	5.
6.	6.
7.	7.
8.	8.
9.	9.
10.	10.
Internal People Analysis	
Weaknesses ("Eliminate/Cope")	**Action**
1.	1.
2.	2.
3.	3.
4.	4.
5.	5.
6.	6.
7.	7.
8.	8.
9.	9.
10.	10.

EXERCISE: (continued)
Final SWOT Analysis—Gaining Consensus

External People Analysis	
Opportunities ("Exploit")	**Action**
1.	1.
2.	2.
3.	3.
4.	4.
5.	5.
6.	6.
7.	7.
8.	8.
9.	9.
10.	10.

External People Analysis	
Threats ("Ease/Lower")	**Action**
1.	1.
2.	2.
3.	3.
4.	4.
5.	5.
6.	6.
7.	7.
8.	8.
9.	9.
10.	10.

Return to your Action Planning analysis. Brainstorm as individuals and fill in the right hand column on this and the previous page—actions are required by each item. Brainstorm at least one action for each item in the left column. It is not necessary to agree on all these actions. They are just initial thoughts to develop core strategies and their actions and priorities (the next step).

STEP #6:
DEVELOPING CORE PEOPLE STRATEGIES

Here we begin to develop Core People Strategies that are aligned to the business needs of the organisation's delivery system, and attuned to the development of people's hearts and minds in support of serving their customers. Both the alignment and attunement strategies should relate closely to each other and support the core strategies of the organisation's overall Strategic Plan.

These Core Strategies enable those who share the responsibility for HR/People Management in an organisation to realise their unique People Edge Vision.

Creating The People Edge – The Systems Thinking Approach To Six People Edge Best Practice Areas

In our extensive human resource research and literature reviews we have identified six Core Strategy Areas that are the major leverage points for Strategic Human Resource Planning. They are based on the Seven Levels of Living Systems that naturally occur on Earth. These levels describe how levels of entities exist and interact.

Systems Levels	**Interactions of Systems Levels**
Level 1—Individuals	**Level 2**—1-to-1/Interpersonal
Level 3—Intact Teams	**Level 4**—Department-to-Department (cross-functional)
Level 5—Organisation-Wide	**Level 6**—Organisation-to-Environment

This leads to the six Core Strategy leverage areas that create the people edge.

Six People Edge Best Practice Areas

Best Practices Research: Over 30 authors researched by the Centre. Here are the results:

Six People Edge Best Practice Areas	Eight Key HR Authors
1. Acquiring the Desired Work Force (Level #1: Self)	1. 6 out of 8 had a similar item
2. Engaging the Work Force (Level #2: One-to-One)	2. 8 out of 8 had a similar item
3. Organising High Performance Teams (Level #3: Teams)	3. 1 out of 8 had a similar item
4. Creating a Learning Organisation (Level #4: Cross-Functional Teams)	4. 5 out of 8 had a similar item
5. Facilitating Cultural Change (Level #5: Organisation-Wide)	5. 5 out of 8 had a similar item
6. Collaborating With Stakeholders (Level #6: Organisation-Environment)	6. 5 out of 8 had a similar item

***Note*:**
- *None had all six competencies.*
- *Only two out of eight even had any of the beginning elements of a systems-oriented approach to strategic human resource management and planning.*

The Centre does not do basic research. We do **action research**. We also summarise and synthesise the research of others. We are translators and interpreters of Best Practices research.

Please Note: The following Six Areas of Best People Practices are available on our online instrument surveys. They will enable you to gather statistical data from a number of people in the organisation. If you are interested, please call the Centre *for* Strategic Management® (San Diego) at (619) 275-6528 or Bandt Gatter & Associates (Australia) at 61-89-322-2877.

Note: *For purposes of developing the Core People Strategies (Step #6) assume that these six areas of Best People Practices are your Core People Strategies.*

Now, let us review what these Core People Strategies are and develop actions under each one that will achieve the Core People Strategies over the next three years.

CORE STRATEGY # 1:
ACQUIRING THE DESIRED WORKFORCE (Individuals)

Organisations across the world are facing a range of challenges in acquiring their desired workforce. Some of these challenges include:

- A rapid growth in the post-50 age group
- A dwindling pool of younger workers
- Talent being increasingly sought after
- Talent becoming shared across organisations
- Retention becoming increasingly difficult
- Greater use being made of technology
- Temporary workers attaining greater prominence

To address these and related issues, Area 1 of the People Edge Practice Model identifies a range of core strategies that need to be considered in the development of "acquisition actions" as part of the Strategic Human Resource/People Plan. These include:

- Identifying core organisational competencies and individual capability requirements
- Developing diverse, flexible, safe and alternative workforce arrangements
- Conducting workforce succession and retention planning
- Implementing recruitment, selection and promotion methods to hire, orient, and assimilate the desired employees
- Exploiting the use of technology as a recruitment tool

EXERCISE: Acquisitions

Individually, list 5 or 6 key "Acquisition" Actions that may be useful within your organisation.

Actions:

EXERCISE: Acquisitions

Compare your "Acquisition" Actions list with your planning team members. Record your agreed-upon list below.

Actions:

CORE STRATEGY # 2:
ENGAGING THE WORKFORCE (Interpersonal, 1-1 Relationships)

Some of the key issues and challenges facing line managers and human resource managers, in terms of engaging the hearts and minds of the workforce, include:

- Retaining good staff is becoming more difficult.
- Managing Baby Boomers continues to present a challenge.
- Managing Generation X and Generation Y workers brings unique challenges.

Some of the key engagement strategies identified in the People Edge Best Practices Model include:

- Installing Performance Management Systems that link individual and team behaviour with strategic direction and core values (i.e., goal setting, coaching, appraisal, development)
- Linking remuneration and compensation systems to capability and performance
- Creating recognition systems that reinforce strategic direction and core values
- Providing flexible benefit programs to meet employer and employee needs
- Dealing effectively with poor or inadequate performance/discipline problems and grievances

EXERCISE: Engaging

List key Actions for "Engaging the Workforce" that might be useful within your organisation.

Actions:

EXERCISE: Engaging

Compare your "Engaging the Workforce" Actions list with your planning team members. Record your agreed-upon list below.

Actions:

CORE STRATEGY # 3:
ORGANISING HIGH PERFORMANCE TEAMS (Intact Teams)

One of the distinctive characteristics of the workplace in the new millennium will be the significant presence of *teams* as a primary model for restructuring and re-organising the way work is completed.

Some of the key strategies that organisations need to consider in developing high performance teams include:

- Understanding, designing and developing task forces and teams
- Developing small-unit team leaders/supervisors
- Developing empowered, self-directed employees, work teams, and accountability
- Establishing participative management skills for management to lead teams in conducting business
- Developing programs that develop team skills and reward and reinforce teamwork

EXERCISE: Teams

List the key Actions for "Organizing High Performance Teams" that might be useful within your organisation.

Actions:

EXERCISE: Teams

Compare your "Organising High Performance Teams" Actions with your planning team members. Record your agreed-upon list below.

Actions:

CORE STRATEGY # 4:
CREATING A LEARNING ORGANISATION (Cross-Functional Teams)

Some of the key learning issues and challenges facing both human resource professionals and line managers include:

- Ensuring that learning is applied to the job
- Ensuring that training is tied to business strategies
- Capturing and transferring knowledge as a critical dimension
- Identifying and building workforce competencies for tomorrow
- Continuing the shift in responsibility for individual learning from the employer to the employee

Some of the key strategies to assist in the creation of a learning organisation include:

- Developing and spreading learning and intellectual capital quickly throughout the organisation
- Institutionalising Systems Thinking as a new approach to better thinking, understanding and acting (KISS: "Simplicity on the far side of complexity")
- Developing Human Resource measurements and information to help the sharing of learning, including cataloguing corporate knowledge
- Promoting the value of debriefing and learning from experiences (mistakes and successes)
- Creating ways to encourage creative thinking and innovation

EXERCISE: Learnings

List the key Actions for creating a "Learning Organisation" that might be useful within your organisation.

Actions:

EXERCISE: Learnings

Compare your creating a "Learning Organisation" Actions list with your planning team members. Record your agreed-upon list below.

Actions:

CORE STRATEGY # 5:
FACILITATING CULTURAL CHANGE (Organisation-wide)

Facilitating and shaping cultural development as a way of creating competitive advantage, and ensuring the development of a desired culture is a major driver in effective organisations. Such organisations increasingly use their culture to create and shape their desired work environment. Market identity is created around the people within the organisation, with the vision and values of the organisation being clearly understood and shared by everyone. This impacts the approach many companies are taking to implement business changes, ensuring that new business practices are consistent with the organisation's values.

Companies are also using cultural change development as the basis for determining the desired behaviours and competencies required of the workforce.

Some of the key strategies that companies need to consider in facilitating cultural change include:

- Engaging in a continuous process of dialogue, discovery and assessment to deepen everyone's shared understanding of the organisation's vision and desired organisation culture vs. its current status
- Shaping and developing collective management skills in support of the desired culture
- Aligning and streamlining all human resource processes, programs and systems with the core values and strategic direction
- Designing and organising structures and people management roles needed to facilitate change to the desired culture
- Developing Strategic Change experts and agents, and broadening the capabilities of all employees to support and implement the desired organisational change

EXERCISE: Culture

List the key Actions for facilitating "Cultural Change" that might be useful within your organisation.

Actions:

EXERCISE: Culture

Compare your facilitating "Cultural Change" Actions with your planning team members. Record your agreed-upon list below.

Actions:

CORE STRATEGY # 6:
COLLABORATING WITH STAKEHOLDERS
(Organisation—Environment)

Business is becoming exceedingly complex as customers and other stakeholders become more refined and more specific in articulating their needs.

As organisations interact more with representatives of multi-national and global organisations, they must develop and acquire the knowledge and skills needed to be successful in a global marketplace. Some of the key strategies to enable this collaboration with key stakeholders include:

- Developing in employees the environmental knowledge, awareness, and skills needed to operate in a global environment
- Understanding, developing, and maintaining strategic alliances and networks, including outsourcing
- Maintaining a positive people environment and competitive advantage in the marketplace
- Creating an intense customer focus and commitment by all employees.
- Collaborating and balancing value contributions to employees, customers, shareholders, community, cultures and countries

EXERCISE: Stakeholders

List the key Actions for "Collaborating with Stakeholders" that might be useful within your organisation.

Actions:

EXERCISE: Stakeholders

Compare your "Collaborating With Stakeholders" Actions with your planning team members. Record your agreed-upon list below.

Actions:

ADDITIONAL PEOPLE EDGE MANAGEMENT STRATEGIES

Are there any additional People Edge Management Strategies your organisation requires other than these six?

Strategies/Actions:

EXERCISE: Consensus List

Getting Consensus on your Human Resource/People Strategies

As a Planning Team, discuss possible priority Human Resource/People Strategies for your Strategic Human Resource/People Plan. List the agreed-upon areas below (Seven maximum—less is better).

Key Strategies
1.
2.
3.
4.
5.
6.
7.

STEP #7:
DEVELOPING YOUR THREE-YEAR PEOPLE EDGE ACTION PLANS – PEOPLE EDGE INTEGRATION

Step #7 involves the development of the Key Actions for the next three years, in support of your Core Strategies.

Then, these Actions are focused down to the top three-to-four "must do" Key Priority Actions for the next year. This leads to the development of a one-year Operational Plan (and eventually a budget) for each major department.

Ideally, it should look like this instead:

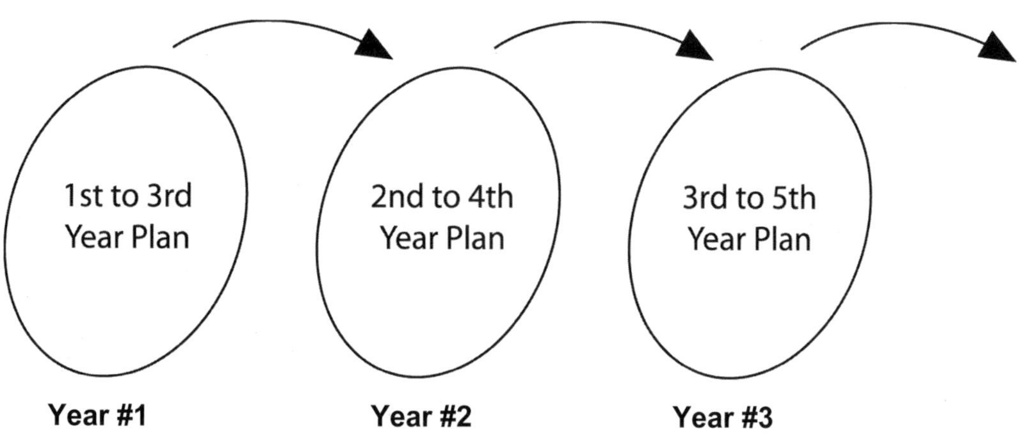

A ROLLING THREE-YEAR PLAN

In many instances in the past, organisations worked hard to prepare multiple-year Strategic Human Resource Plans which outline the key initiatives to be undertaken over the next three, four, or five years. This exercise is often viewed as a major task assignment, and once it has been prepared, people believe it is to be followed religiously, regardless of what's happening in the rest of the world.

In reality, the external and internal influences that any organisation must confront on a continual basis, from month-to-month and year-to-year, will demand continuous updates and modifications to your plan. These cannot be viewed as "static plans." To be effective in meeting changing customer expectations, these plans must be seen, and be treated, as a "dynamic game plan."

Visually, it could look like this:

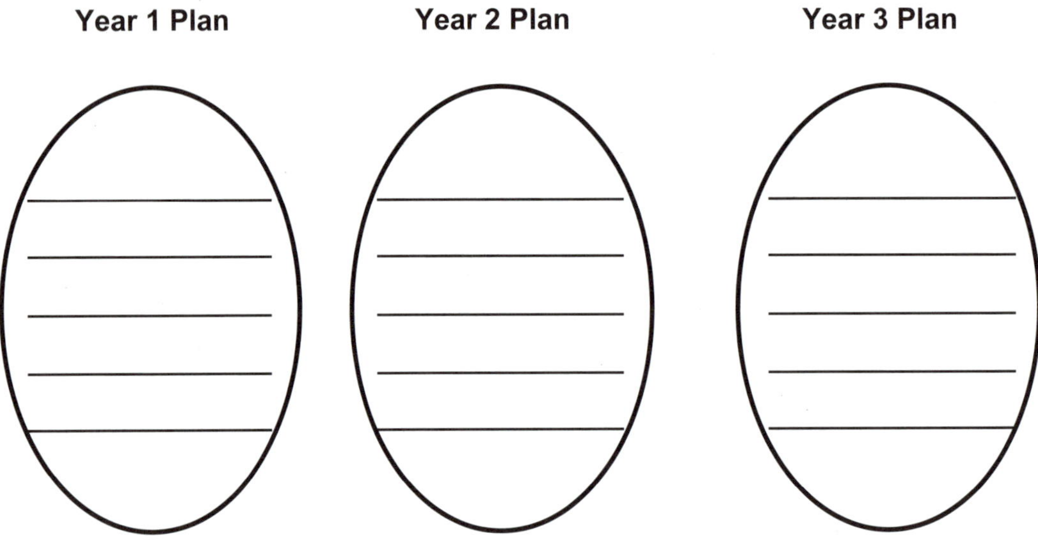

Using this traditional plan, after the first 9-12 months of your three-year Plan have expired, you are left with a two-year Plan, and then ultimately a one-year Plan. This approach requires a major exercise in preparing the initial plan, with subsequent attention to the planning process (waning over the next three years), followed by a major redraft and a new Three-Year Plan, once the initial plan has run its course.

There is a better way to keep this planning relevant, and to maintain the organisation's interest and motivation from one year to the next. Here it is:

A more effective approach is to establish the rhythm of an annual process for developing the next year's plan, adjusting that year's plan and adding a new year-three component. This creates the notion of a *continuous* "Three-Year Rolling Plan" process.

Through this approach, you will need to set aside time each year to:

- Review your progress for the current year;
- Review and update plans for years two and three, then roll them forward into years one and two; and
- Identify the next phase of new initiatives, or the next phases of some longer-term strategies, which becomes your *new* year-three plan.

This process will create a systematic approach in which you are "continuously managing your business in a strategic way." It allows for maximum flexibility, without losing focus and direction. It sets up a new rhythm for how you run your business.

SAMPLE THREE-YEAR PEOPLE PLAN

Strategy: Management & Leadership	**Year 1**	**Year 2**	**Year 3**
Actions:			
1 Implement a corporate development program to build superior performance in core competencies, based on individual learning contracts.	X		
2. Develop a best practice process for the recruitment of managers and executives, using core competencies as a basis.	X		
3. Obtain executive agreement on the desired mix of internal/external recruitment.		X	
4. Develop a succession planning process that identifies management potential and prepares individuals for senior management positions.			X
5. Implement multi-rater (360°) appraisals for managers and executives.			X

Note: *You can pull many of your actions for Step #7 from our Six Best Practices People Areas on the previous pages or from our SWOT analysis. However, consider these carefully and avoid simply copying answers from there to here.*

Now, on the next few pages, let's develop your Rolling Three-Year Actions under each of the Core Strategies.

EXERCISE: Core Strategy #1: ______________________________
Developing Your Human Resource/People Actions

Collectively, list below your possible priority Human Resource/People Actions for Years 1, 2 and 3 of your Strategic Human Resource/People Plan. Place an X in the column for the relevant year.

Core Strategy and Actions	Lead Accountability	Year 1	Year 2	Year 3
Strategy #1 : ____________________ ______________________________ Actions: 1. 2. 3. 4. 5. 6. 7. 8. 9. 10.				

Remember: Select the top 2-4 action priorities for the first year's leverage points.

EXERCISE: Core Strategy #2: ________________________________

Developing Your Human Resource Actions

Collectively, list below your possible priority Human Resource Actions for Years 1, 2, and 3 of your Strategic Human Resource/People Plan. Place an X in the column for the relevant year.

Core Strategy and Actions	**Lead Accountability**	**Year 1**	**Year 2**	**Year 3**
Strategy #2 : ______________________ ______________________________ Actions: 1. 2. 3. 4. 5. 6. 7. 8. 9. 10.				

Remember: Select the top 2-4 action priorities for the first year's leverage points.

EXERCISE: Core Strategy #3: ______________________________
Developing Your Human Resource Actions

Collectively list below your possible priority Human Resource Actions for Years 1, 2, and 3 of your Strategic Human Resource/People Plan. Place an X in the column for the relevant year.

Core Strategy and Actions	Lead Accountability	Year 1	Year 2	Year 3
Strategy #3 : ______________________ ______________________ Actions: 1. 2. 3. 4. 5. 6. 7. 8. 9. 10.				

Remember: Select the top 2-4 action priorities for the first year's leverage points.

EXERCISE: Core Strategy #4: ______________________________

Developing Your Human Resource Actions

Collectively list below your possible priority Human Resource Actions for Years 1, 2, and 3 of your Strategic Human Resource/People Plan. Place an X in the column for the relevant year.

Core Strategy and Action	Lead Accountability	Year 1	Year 2	Year 3
Strategy #4 :______________________ ______________________________ Actions: 1. 2. 3. 4. 5. 6. 7. 8. 9. 10.				

Remember: Select the top 2-4 action priorities for the first year's leverage points.

EXERCISE: Core Strategy #5: ______________________________

Developing Your Human Resource Actions

Collectively list below your possible priority Human Resource Actions for Years 1, 2, and 3 of your Strategic Human Resource/People Plan. Place an X in the column for the relevant year.

Core Strategy and Actions	Lead Accountability	Year 1	Year 2	Year 3
Strategy #5 :______________________ ______________________________				
Actions:				
1.				
2.				
3.				
4.				
5.				
6.				
7.				
8.				
9.				
10.				

Remember: Select the top 2-4 action priorities for the first year's leverage points.

EXERCISE: Core Strategy #6: ______________________________

Developing Your Human Resource Actions

Collectively list below your possible priority Human Resource Actions for Years 1, 2, and 3 of your Strategic Human Resource/People Plan. Place an X in the column for the relevant year.

Core Strategy and Actions	Lead Accountability	Year 1	Year 2	Year 3
Strategy #6 :______________________ ______________________________ Actions: 1. 2. 3. 4. 5. 6. 7. 8. 9. 10.				

Remember: Select the top 2-4 action priorities for the first year's leverage points.

EXERCISE: Core Strategy #7: ______________________________

Developing Your Human Resource Actions

Collectively list below your possible priority Human Resource Actions for Years 1, 2, and 3 of your Strategic Human Resource/People Plan. Place an X in the column for the relevant year.

Core Strategy and Actions	Lead Accountability	Year 1	Year 2	Year 3
Strategy #7 :______________________ ______________________________ Actions: 1. 2. 3. 4. 5. 6. 7. 8. 9. 10.				

Remember: Select the top 2-4 action priorities for the first year's leverage points.

"The Devil is in the Details" – Work Plans

One of the many reasons that Strategic Human Resource/People Planning fails is that we do not sufficiently specify: the work tasks that are necessary to implement the plan; who is responsible for implementing the tasks; and when the implementation should occur.

This is why Work Planning is so important in the process. It is the development of specific tasks necessary to ensure the implementation of each of the priority strategies during the next twelve months.

Remember the Key Work Planning Questions (to implement the people strategies):

- What are the specific tasks that need to occur?
- Who in the team or organisation should be responsible?
- When will the tasks need to be undertaken? When Completed?

Sample Work Plan			
STRATEGY	**Managing Performance**		
First Year Actions:	Implement a revised performance management scheme that: • Reflects competencies arising from workforce planning exercise • Is results-oriented • Reflects the organisational change agenda • Considers 360° feedback		
Work Plan	**Who**	**When**	**Progress**
1. Establish a partnering steering committee.	HR Manager & Corporate HR	August	
2. Identify pilot sites for implementation (based upon competency work).	HR Manager/ Consultant	August	
3. Review current performance planning and review and research best practice.	Performance Consultant	September	
4. Develop the proposed performance management process including: • Policy, systems, processes, training	Performance Consultant	September	
5. Obtain feedback and sign off other Senior Managers for proposed changes.	HR Manager	October	
6. Conduct awareness sessions on the proposed process for staff in pilot sites.	T&D staff	November	
7. Conduct training for managers and staff in all pilot sites.	T&D staff	November	
8. Implement pilot sites.	Performance Consultant	November	
9. Develop a strategy to "roll out" the pilot program to the remainder of organisation.	Performance Consultant	December	
10. Evaluate the pilot program.	Performance Consultant	April	

EXERCISE: Work Plan Development

Complete the following work plan for one of your Core Strategies.

Note: Copy this as many times as necessary to build your work plans.

STRATEGY (list one):		
First Year Action *(list one):*		
My Unit's Work Plan	**Who**	**When**
1.		
2.		
3.		
4.		

PART III

IMPLEMENTATION AND CHANGE

PHASES 

PHASE D: IMPLEMENTATION & CHANGE

"Effective change takes 3-5 years to bring about, even with concentrated and continued actions."
—Stephen G. Haines

STEP #8:
PLAN-TO-IMPLEMENT

Proper planning prevents poor performance

As outlined at the beginning of this book, successful Strategic Human Resource Planning is not just about developing a Plan; it is also about successfully implementing it! This section focuses upon the specifics of how to implement your Strategic Human Resource/People Plan—Plan-to-Implement.

In Step #8 you develop a one-year implementation plan which outlines, in very practical terms, the steps, processes and structures required for successful implementation.

This includes how the plan will be communicated and how the change process will be managed and coordinated. The key element is regular follow-up by a group, such as the People Executive/Employee Development Board mentioned in Step #1. They maintain and continually refine the Plan as a living, breathing document.

EXERCISE: Implementation Problems

Why Strategic Human Resource/People Planning Implementation Fails
Research and experience shows that strategy implementation fails for many reasons, including the following commonly identified problems on the next page.

IMPLEMENTATION PROBLEMS

As a Planning Team, summarise from your own lists those areas where attention is needed to implement your Strategic Human Resource/People Plan.

Most common problems encountered	**Attention required?** (✓ Check)
1. Time required to implement changes was underestimated.	
2. Major problems surfaced during implementation that had not been identified beforehand.	
3. Uncontrollable factors in the external environment had an adverse impact on implementation.	
4. Competing activities and crises distracted management from implementing the decision.	
5. The plan was not communicated adequately throughout organisation.	
6. Coordination of implementation activities was not effective enough.	
7. Key implementation tasks and activities were not defined in sufficient detail: • the actual work required to implement strategies • who would be involved and accountable for each task • how long each task would take • what resources would be needed	
8. Processes for monitoring and reporting progress were not defined.	
9. Leadership and direction provided by department managers were not effective.	
10. Capabilities of employees involved were not sufficient.	
11. Business control systems, such as performance measurement, budgets, and human resource information, were not realigned to support the new strategies.	
12. Information systems used to monitor implementation were inadequate.	

Now: **Build an Action Plan on the next page to ensure that these key problems don't happen to you.**

Action Plan for Implementation Problems

What	Who	When

Rollercoaster of Change^{SM}

Effective Strategic Human Resource/People Planning results in significant individual, team and organisational change. For this reason, it is important for those associated with Strategic Human Resource Planning to understand and manage the strategic change process.

The first thing to appreciate is how we experience change. The Rollercoaster of Change^{SM} diagram simplifies and clarifies the basic psychology of individual and organisational change.

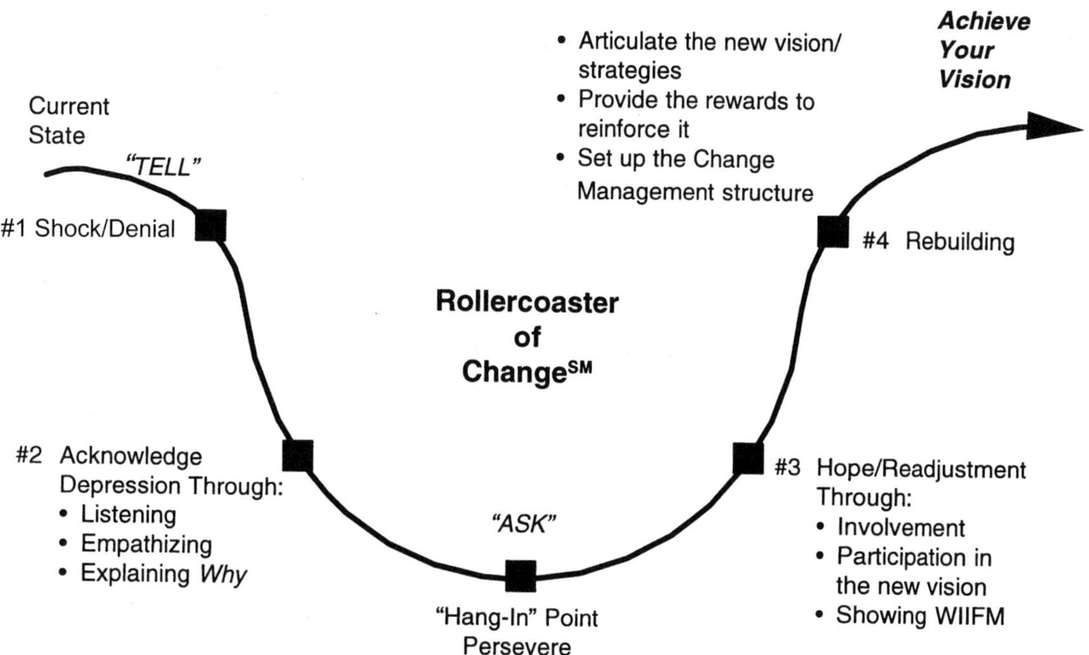

EXERCISE:

Study this model's four basic steps, keeping in mind that the reality of change is much more complex. Each employee goes through this at his or her own pace and depth, in a process that must be managed. Individuals often undergo a number of different changes at the same time (personal, professional, social and spiritual).

Focus on the bottoming-out point, where success or failure is often decided. When times get tough, perseverance and discipline in your thinking and acting are needed.

QUESTIONS TO ADDRESS
Rollercoaster of Change^{SM}

There are major questions that you should keep in mind when implementing major change. ***Discuss these questions fully with your planning team and your other key stakeholders.***

1. Not "if" but "when" will we start to go through shock/depression?
2. How deep is the trough? Is it different for each person? What are the implications?
3. How long does the trough take? Are employees and management at the same stage of change at the same time?
4. Will we hang in and persevere to get past the bottom? How?
5. How do we manage change proactively?
6. At what level will we rebuild?
7. Will we rebuild and fully achieve our vision?
8. What new skills do we need to accomplish this?
9. How many different rollercoasters will we experience in this change?
10. Are there other changes occurring at the same time for people?
11. How will we deal with normal resistance?
12. How will we create a critical mass to support and achieve the desired changes?

EXERCISE:
Rollercoaster of Change^{SM}

List below some of the change management issues that you are likely to encounter and your tactics for dealing with them when implementing your Strategic Human Resource/People Plan.

COMMUNICATING THE STRATEGIC HR/PEOPLE PLAN

Successful communication and marketing of the plan to your key internal stakeholders is imperative to ensure its effective implementation. Listed below are some ideas to accomplish this.

EXERCISE:

Check the ones important for you to do.

- Print the plan and distribute it to all employees, along with a cover letter from the CEO and the Director of Human Resources.
- Develop a set of handouts, overhead slides, or a slide presentation for "standard use" by all executives and managers.
- Hold meetings with managers as a group to hear from the CEO and the Director of Human Resources about the plan's impact on how the Human Resource element of the business will be handled in the future.
- Hold work unit/work team meetings with managers to examine the impact on staff, and allow staff to ask questions about the plan and pose their own concerns.
- Conduct meetings with key stakeholders to review results; thank them for their help; and discuss potential impacts on stakeholders.
- Conduct two-day workshops for managers to introduce the new model of Human Resource Management and to discuss how their own management practices will need to change.
- Establish direct "customer contact links" between Human Resource staff and line managers to assist with the implementation aspects of the plan.
- Develop posters that depict the "New Workplace Culture" that you are creating.
- Produce a videotape of key players outlining the overall Human Resource vision. Include comments from line managers and employees discussing the impacts as they see them.
- Set up a website for Strategic Human Resources and progress reports.
- Publish internal HR newsletters to keep people posted on the plan's implementation progress—the successes, breakdowns and modifications—over the first 12-18 months.
- Circulate the "report card results" of your "Key People Success Measures" each quarter and share these with all your stakeholders.

Now–how to keep the plan alive over the next 3–5 years?

SAMPLE TEMPLATE Communication Plan

Action	Who	When
1. Print a one-page summary of the plan, with a cover letter. • Distribute to members of staff • Distribute to managers and program heads		
2. Conduct across-department meetings to hear directly from the Director and other members of the Planning Team. (Also thank them for their help.)		
3. Hold meetings of staff within departments to ask questions about the plan and raise any concerns.		
4. Meet with key stakeholders and discuss the plan. Provide complete plan.		
5. Develop a poster with the vision, mission, values and goals.		
6. Publish an internal newsletter outlining progress following the HR Planning Team Review.		
7. Publish a "report card" of progress after the 6-month review; distribute to all stakeholders.		
8. Establish a schedule to meet with each Department Manager over the next 12 months. • Determine their needs and expectations • Outline HR's strategic direction and services		
9. Establish a website that details strategic people management plans, products, services, and contacts.		
10. Prepare a brochure outlining strategic people management plan and products and services.		
11. Ensure that three articles are published in the company magazine each year, outlining Strategic HR accomplishments.		
12. Undertake extensive consultations one month before the next strategic planning exercise.		

EXERCISE: Communication Plan

List below the specific actions that you will undertake to communicate your Strategic Human Resource/People Plan. Discuss with your Planning Team and revise where necessary.

THREE MECHANISMS
FOR SUCCESSFUL IMPLEMENTATION

Three extremely successful mechanisms will improve the chances for effective implementation, build line management / Human Resource partnerships, and gain employee involvement.
These mechanisms are:

1: Establishing an Employee Development Board

2: Establishing HR/People Strategy Sponsor Teams

3: Establishing HR/People Plan Review Meetings

Mechanism #1: Employee Development Board (or subcommittee thereof)

A new way to implement your Strategic HR/People Plan is to give equal weight to managing desired changes, in addition to the daily management of ongoing HR/People practices and activities. If you have not already established the Employee Development Board, now is the time to do so.

Purpose

- To monitor, guide and track the overall process of implementing the Strategic HR/People Plan, including Key Success Measures
- To coordinate any other major performance improvement projects going on in the organisation at the same time
- To ensure a seamless fit with the demands of ongoing daily HR business activities

Committee Meeting Frequency

Phase I: Monthly or bi-monthly as the process begins

Phase II: Quarterly, once the process is functioning smoothly

Suggested Membership

- HR Executive
- One or more members of the Executive Team
- One or more line managers who share your "vision for Human Resource and people management" and are willing to actively support it
- Informal or formal organisation leaders that are key to implementation
- Members of the HR team who will be leading major change processes
- The person responsible for tracking Key People Success Measures

This is an ideal way to build a
Strategic Human Resource Staff/Line Management
Business Partnership

EXERCISE: Employee Development Board

Designing Your Employee Development Board

Individually, list your views about the purpose, membership and meeting frequency of your Board. Add to/ revise your list after discussions with the Planning Team.

Outline the purposes of your Employee Development Board
Membership
Frequency of Meetings

Standard Agenda Items:	**Frequency:**
1. Key People Success Measures Review	1.
2. First Year's Priority Action List (top 2-4 per strategy)	2.
3. Action Plans	3.
4. Environmental Scan	4.
5. Internal Communications	5.
6. Strategy Sponsorship Teams (see next page)	6.

Mechanism #2: HR/People Strategy Sponsor Teams

A new way to implement your Strategic HR/People Plan is to give equal weight to managing desired changes, in addition to the daily management of ongoing HR/People practices and activities.

Purpose

- To ensure cross-functional interest and attention towards implementing the HR/People strategies
- To provide a dedicated interest group for each major people strategy
- To oversee the development of action plans for the strategy and implementation of these plans
- To zealously monitor and track the implementation efforts and results of the human resource strategy
- To provide updates for the Employee Development Board (or sub-committee thereof) at each of their quarterly meetings

Strategy Sponsor Team Meeting Frequency

Phase I: Bi-weekly or monthly, until action plans have been completed and implementation has commenced.

Phase II: As needed, once implementation is well underway.

Team Membership: (keep to 6 maximum)

- A member of senior management to serve as Team Leader
- One dedicated staff member from the corporate HR Department who has a keen interest in the particular HR/People strategy that this team is to monitor
- Two or three line managers who have an interest in this strategy
- Two or three front line staff members (from different business units) to contribute from an employee perspective and ensure that the "pulse of the organisation" is monitored throughout the change process

This is an ideal way to build cross-functional involvement in the implementation of your Strategic HR/People Plan

EXERCISE: HR/People Strategy Sponsor Team #1

Designing Your HR/People Strategy Sponsor Team

Individually, list your views about the purpose, membership and meeting frequency of one of your Sponsor Teams. Add to/ revise your list after discussions with the Planning Team.

Question: Do you want one Sponsor Team per strategy?

Outline the purposes of this HR/People Strategy Sponsor Team #1
Membership
Frequency of Meetings

EXERCISE: HR/People Strategy Sponsor Team #2

Designing Your HR/People Strategy Sponsor Team

Individually, list your views about the purpose, membership and meeting frequency of one of your Sponsor Teams. Add to/ revise your list after discussions with the Planning Team.

Outline the purposes of this HR/People Strategy Sponsor Team #2
Membership
Frequency of Meetings

EXERCISE: HR/People Strategy Sponsor Team #3

Designing your HR/People Strategy Sponsor Team

Individually, list your views about the purpose, membership and meeting frequency of one of your Sponsor Teams. Add to/ revise your list after discussions with the Planning Team.

Outline the purposes of this HR/People Strategy Sponsor Team #3
Membership
Frequency of Meetings

Mechanism #3 HR/People Plan Review Meetings

Purpose

- To assess the progress and results of the Strategic Human Resource/People Plan implementation process on a quarterly basis
- To adjust and modify the various phases of implementation as needed to ensure that the integrity and intention of the plan is maintained
- To initiate the Annual Strategic HR/People Plan's Review (and Update) process (This will usually occur at the third quarterly meeting, which allows time for final refinements before the year-end and time to prepare for the next year's budget process.)

Meeting Frequency

- At first, once every month or two to ensure a proper "kick off"
- Once every three months (Obtain confirmation of, and commitment to, specific dates at the start of each year.)

Participants

- All members of the Employee Development Board
- Also possibly:
  - The Team Leaders for each of the HR/People Strategy Sponsor Teams
  - Key members of the Corporate HR Department
  - Selected Key Stakeholders/Sponsor Team members as needed

EXERCISE: Review Meetings

Designing Your HR/People Plan Review Meetings

Individually, list your views about the purpose, membership and meeting frequency of your Quarterly HR/People Plan Review Meetings. Add to/ revise your list after discussions with the Planning Team.

Outline the purposes of your Review Meetings
Frequency of Meetings
Participants
1. Employee Development Board Members
2.
3.

EXERCISE: Sample HR/People Planning Document

Use the prototype below to review and finalise your Strategic Human Resource/People Planning document for use in a practical day-to-day fashion.

I. INTRODUCTION

1. Cover Sheet
2. Executive Summary
3. Strategic People Planning Model
4. Acknowledgments
5. Table of Contents

II. BUSINESS SCANNING & STRATEGIC ISSUES

1. Environmental Issues
2. Strategic Direction of Organisation
3. Distinctive Competencies
4. Key People Management Capabilities/New Roles
5. Key Human Resource Issues

III. IDEAL FUTURE VISION & STRATEGIES

A

{ 1 People Edge Vision
{ 2. Mission (for Human Resource Department)
{ 3. Core Values – for the Organisation

B

4. Key People Success Measures

C

{ 5. Current State People Assessment
{ 6. Core People Strategies
{ 7. Rolling Three-Year Plans
{ 8. Annual Top Priority Actions for Year 1

D

9. Work Plan for Year 1

IV. IMPLEMENTATION

1. Communication Plan
2. Implementation Plan

Note: *To Order a* **Strategic HR/People Planning Document Template***:*
Website: www.systemsthinkingpress.com, *or*
Email to info@systemsthinkingpress.com, *or*
Call (619) 275-6528 in the USA

STEP #9:
STRATEGY IMPLEMENTATION AND CHANGE

Step #9 is the point of actual implementation, completion of tasks and priorities, and period of adjusting actions, as needed, during the year.

It also involves managing the change process, measuring progress against the Key People Success Factors and celebrating achievements along the way.

What does your yearly comprehensive calendar/map look like? Be sure to include time for next year's budgeting and Annual Strategic Human Resource/People Plan Review and Update (see next page).

YEARLY COMPREHENSIVE MAP		
Month	**Date**	**Meeting Type/Process Point**
January		
February		
March		
April		
May		
June		
July		
August		
September		
October		
November		
December		

STEP #10:
ANNUAL STRATEGIC HR/PEOPLE PLAN REVIEW AND UPDATE

Organisations are facing continuous change, requiring planners to place additional emphasis upon continual environmental scanning and review.

We recommend a "mini environmental scan" every six months, as a minimum, as well as having it conducted as part of the Annual Strategic People Plan Review & Update each year.

This is similar to a yearly independent financial audit. It has two goals:

Goal #1: Assess the status of how well your Strategic People Plan has been achieved.

Goal #2: Assess the implementation of your system of planning and managing change.

This review has five main tasks:

Task #1: Reacting to changes in the environment and their implications for updating your plan.

Task #2: Verifying your vision, mission, and core values, and rechecking your key success factors and core strategies.

Task #3: Updating annual Human Resource action priorities for the next 12 months for each core people strategy.

Task #4: Holding the annual large group review meeting on the new plan.

Task #5: Updating your Employee Development Board's plan for success and its system for managing change for the next year.

At this point, you should have developed an excellent Strategic Human Resource/People Plan for your organisation. Now, your main "planning task" is to review and update it annually only as necessary, not redo it. It is crucial to strategically manage the Plan you have created.

What is your game plan for accomplishing the above five tasks?

What (Tasks #1-#5)	Lead Accountability	When
1.		
2.		
3.		
4.		
5.		

ANNUAL HR/PEOPLE REVIEW AND UPDATE

Based on the framework below (#1 and #2), each organisation needs to conduct a yearly follow-up and diagnosis of how they are performing. This is key to "learning to be a high-performance organisation" by using our three goals 1) Planning, 2) Implementation, and 3) Annual Updates as an integrated "Strategic Management System".

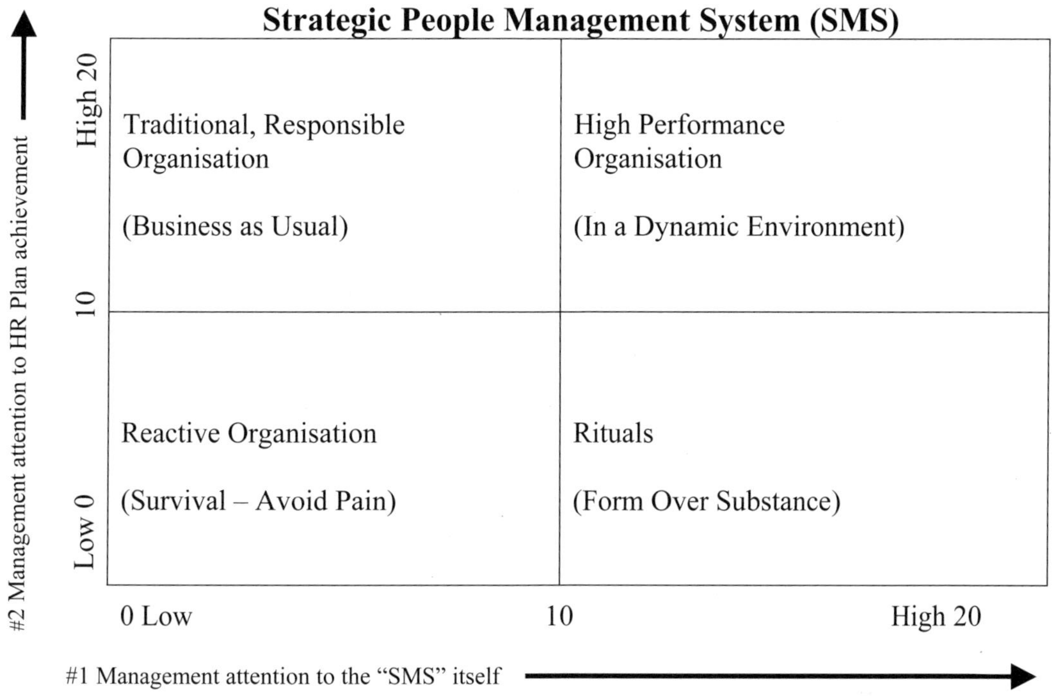

Strategic People Management System (SMS)

#2 Management attention to HR Plan achievement →		
High 20	Traditional, Responsible Organisation (Business as Usual)	High Performance Organisation (In a Dynamic Environment)
10		
Low 0	Reactive Organisation (Survival – Avoid Pain)	Rituals (Form Over Substance)
	0 Low	10 High 20

#1 Management attention to the "SMS" itself →

Summary

It is important for organisations to develop Strategic Human Resource/People Plans for their businesses. However, once these plans are developed, it is crucial to have a system of strategically managing implementation of these plans.

Hence, the last piece of our *Successful Strategic Human Resource Planning* book goes by the name of: *Strategic People Management System* (SMS). All of your pre-work, planning, implementing, and updating goals combine to produce this three-part Strategic People Management System—the new way to effectively manage your most important asset—your people.

For a visual representation of this Strategic People Management System, see the diagram on the next page.

STRATEGIC PEOPLE MANAGEMENT SYSTEM (SMS)

"CREATING PEOPLE AS YOUR COMPETITIVE BUSINESS ADVANTAGE"

"Thinking Backwards To Your Future" The Systems Thinking Approach℠

THREE GOALS: STRATEGIC PEOPLE MANAGEMENT SYSTEM

GOAL I: ***DEVELOP A STRATEGIC PLAN/DOCUMENT***	***(PHASES A, B, C)***
STEP #1: Plan-to-Plan (Educate and Organise for Planning)	
✓ Organisational Diagnosis	
✓ Executive Briefing	
✓ Plan-to-Plan Tasks	
✓ Visionary Leadership and Team Building (optional)	
STEPS #2 – #7: Strategic Planning	
✓ Conduct Strategic Planning	
✓ Core Strategies	
✓ Rolling 3-year Plan	
✓Annual Plans / Budgets	
GOAL II: ***ENSURE SUCCESSFUL IMPLEMENTATION & CHANGE***	***(PHASE D)***
STEP #8: Plan-to-Implement (Educate and Organise for Change)	
✓ Rollercoaster of Change[SM]	
✓ Communicating the Plan	
✓ Three Mechanisms for Effective Implementation	
STEP #9: Strategy, Implementation and Change	
✓ Implementing Strategic Change	
✓ Yearly Comprehensive Map	
GOAL III: ***BUILD AND SUSTAIN HIGH PERFORMANCE—LONG TERM***	***(PHASES A, B, C, D, E)***
STEP #10: Annual Strategic HR/People Plan Review (& Update)	
✓ Annual Strategic Review (and Update): Independent Evaluation	
✓ Increased Team Building and Leadership Development (optional)	
Bottom Line: ***Create and Sustain a People Edge as a High-Performance Organisation***	

www.SystemsThinkingPress.com

Premier Publishers and Clearinghouse for Systems Thinking Resources

619-275-6528

We offer a complete line of Strategic Human Resource Management Products, all based on our Systems Thinking Approach^{SM}.

CURRENT PROVEN PRODUCTS
Used by Consultants and Trainers of the Centre for Strategic Management®.

1. Successful Strategic Human Resource Planning
2. Strategic People Edge Planning Participant Notebook (for HR Planning or Training)
3. Template to build you own Strategic Human Resource/People Plan
4. Executive Briefing Booklet on Strategic Human Resource Planning
5. 4-Colour Model on Strategic Human Resource Planning
6. 4-Page Executive Summary Article on Creating the People Edge
7. Two Volumes of Master Tool Kits and Guides on all aspects of Strategic Human Resource Planning and Management (500 pages each) a virtual Ph.D. in HR
8. Succession Management Guide (Planning and Development)
9. Organisational Assessment – HR Best People Practices (online or hardcopy)
10. Tailored Employee Values/Satisfaction Surveys (choose from over 1500 questions)

NEW PRODUCTS

Our product line is continually growing. Ask us for our newest selections, all based on our Systems Thinking Approach^{SM}.

A Global Alliance of Master Consultants and Trainers
www.csmintl.com